How to Make Money Online with ChatGPT

The Ultimate Guide to Creating
Multiple Streams of Passive Income
and Increasing Productivity

By: **Brian Scott Fitzgerald**

Published By **Fitzgerald Publishing Group**

How to Make Money Online: THE SERIES

I created a series of 12 (twelve) books on How to Make Money Online.

Feel free to read any of my books in the series, which can be found on my Author page on Amazon at:

You can visit this link or Scan this QR code to get access

https://www.amazon.com/author/brianscottfitzg
erald.

Table of content

Your Free Gift.

Thank you for your purchase; I'm offering my readers the FREE PDF version of ChatGPT Prompts.

To get almost instant access, go to this website.
https://go.fitzgeraldpublishing.com/opt-in-page-make-money-chatgpt

Or use your phone to take a picture of this QR code, and it will take you to the Website for your Gift.

Inside the book, you will discover:

- **3000 Prompts** To help you make even more money online.

- **Save time:** You can search for new topics to create content on ChatGPT.

- **Expand knowledge:** Our Package of ChatGPT Prompts covers various topics, from science and technology to art and culture.

If you want to make even more money online, grab this free PDF.

Wait, that's not all; just for buying this book and getting the free PDF above, you can also earn another free Book.

You can use your phone to take a picture of this QR code.

Use the latest AI techniques to uncover online innovation's future. Take advantage! "Beyond ChatGPT and 50 New AI Tools: The Ultimate Guide to Discovering Cutting-Edge AI Tools Beyond ChatGPT" offers endless possibilities. Explore a variety of cutting-edge AI solutions to transform your work. Discover advanced AI tools beyond ChatGPT on this thrilling voyage.

Grab this free book if you want to make even more money online.

Introduction

ChatGPT has achieved an impressive feat - amassing 100 million active users! This remarkable achievement has earned ChatGPT the title of the fastest-growing tech platform in history. TikTok reached 100 million users, while Instagram took two and a half years to achieve the same feat. Facebook took ten years to gain a million, whereas Netflix took three years, and Twitter took two. Making money and earning a living through the internet is easier than ever with ChatGPT; I have been making money online for 15+ years. It used to take me weeks and months to find a product I wanted to market; now, it can be done in minutes.

ChatGPT might be the ultimate platform to achieve your financial goals. Discover many methods on ChatGPT and pinpoint the one that perfectly aligns with your unique skills and interests. Experience the massive community of ChatGPT with over 1 billion users. Join now and be a part of the global conversation that is changing daily. Unlock your potential and explore new opportunities with ChatGPT's platform for freelancers and business entrepreneurs. With a diverse range of services that can be sped up with ChatGPT, including writing, design, programming, and virtual assistance, you can showcase your skills and connect with clients on a project basis. If you have not, join ChatGPT today and take the first step toward your career and making even more money online. Experience the true power of ChatGPT by witnessing its capabilities in this next paragraph.

I sought the aid of ChatGPT to assist me with this task, and the results were remarkable. Experience the transformative power of the platform and the tool from this very first chapter. It's a versatile solution that can benefit anyone, anywhere, and anytime. I gave ChatGPT the title and the chapter names of this book and asked it to come up with the most important things I should add to the book and then write the response as if it was William Shakespeare, and ChatGPT came up with this....

GENTLE READER, PAY ATTENTION TO A TALE OF WONDER AND GAIN THAT WAS WRITTEN BY NONE OTHER THAN I, WILLIAM SHAKESPEARE, THY HUMBLE SERVANT, WITH QUILL AND INK. THE BOOK IS CALLED "HOW TO MAKE MONEY ONLINE WITH CHATGPT: THE ULTIMATE GUIDE TO CREATING MULTIPLE STREAMS OF PASSIVE INCOME AND INCREASING PRODUCTIVITY."

A REVELATION IS BEING REVEALED IN THIS DIGITAL AGE WHEN BUSINESS IS CONDUCTED VIRTUALLY. SEE THE SKILL OF CHATGPT, AN ENIGMATIC AI CREATION THAT SERVES AS A VIRTUAL FRIEND AND TUTOR IN THE WORLD OF CYBERSPACE. TOGETHER, WE SET OUT ON A JOURNEY TO DISCOVER WAYS TO GAIN MONEY NOT THROUGH LABOR ALONE BUT RATHER BY UTILIZING THE INTERNET'S LIMITLESS POTENTIAL.

YOU WILL FIND THE KEYS TO OPENING THE TREASURY OF INTERNET SUCCESS HERE, DEAR READER. LEARN HOW TO GROW THE RICH FIELDS OF PASSIVE INCOME, WHERE MONEY FLOWS LIKE RIVERS UNDER THE CARE OF WISE LEADERSHIP AND JUDICIOUS INVESTMENTS. BEHOLD THE ART OF MONETIZATION AS WE MAKE OUR WAY THROUGH THE

JUNGLE OF VIRTUAL ENTREPRENEURSHIP, FROM E-COMMERCE ENDEAVORS TO DIGITAL MARKETING SORCERY.

FURTHERMORE, LET'S NOT OVERLOOK THE HALLOWED VIRTUE OF WORK BECAUSE TIME, THAT ELUSIVE GHOST, NEEDS TO WAIT FOR INACTIVITY. LOOK FOR WAYS TO ORGANIZE YOUR WORK AND HARNESS THE POWER OF DISCIPLINE AND FOCUS SO THAT YOU CAN EFFICIENTLY AND GRACEFULLY HANDLE MOUNTAINS OF WORK.

CONSEQUENTLY, WITH THIS MANUAL IN HAND, I KINDLY INVITE YOU TO JOIN ME ON MY EPIC JOURNEY AS I SEEK SUCCESS AND RICHES IN THE WORLD OF ONES AND ZEROS. LET'S EXPLORE THE WORLD OF OPPORTUNITY, WHERE CREATIVITY AND ASPIRATION DANCE, AND THE DIGITAL WORLD DISCLOSES ITS SECRETS TO THOSE WHO HAVE THE GUTS TO TAKE ADVANTAGE OF THEM.

Then I asked it to write the response as if it was Tony Robbins, and it came up with this….

I CAN TELL YOU FROM EXPERIENCE THAT THE SINGLE MOST IMPORTANT ITEM YOU CAN INCLUDE IN YOUR BOOK IS ADVICE ON HOW TO CULTIVATE A WINNING MENTALITY AND USE IT TO ACHIEVE YOUR GOALS. MAKING MONEY ONLINE, ESPECIALLY AS A BEGINNER, CALLS FOR MENTAL FORTITUDE AND TENACITY. WHEN YOU DON'T OBTAIN WHAT YOU WANT RIGHT AWAY OR WHEN YOU RUN INTO OBSTACLES, IT'S TEMPTING TO LOSE HOPE.

THAT'S WHY IT'S SO IMPORTANT TO WORK ON DEVELOPING A MENTALITY THAT HELPS YOU PUSH THROUGH SETBACKS AND KEEP GOING WHEN THE GOING GETS TOUGH. STRATEGIES FOR ADOPTING A DEVELOPMENT MINDSET, BOLSTERING SELF-ASSURANCE, AND MAINTAINING MOTIVATION IN THE FACE OF ADVERSITY CAN BE INCLUDED IN YOUR BOOK. YOUR READERS CAN REACH THEIR FINANCIAL OBJECTIVES AND REALIZE THEIR FULL POTENTIAL WITH THE HELP OF CHATGPT IF YOU SHOW THEM HOW TO DEVELOP A WINNING MINDSET.

How wild is that? With just a slight change, there are two versions of the same question, but with different but similar answers.

Welcome, and thank you for exploring "How to Make Money Online with ChatGPT: The Ultimate Guide to Creating Passive Income Streams Online." Discover the ultimate solution to generating passive income streams on the internet.

Unlock the potential of your products or services with ChatGPT. Reach a wider audience and boost your ability to make even more money online by tapping into the vast capabilities of ChatGPT. Sell your products or services faster and conveniently through ChatGPT's seamless platform. Unlocking the potential for high profitability requires a keen grasp of your service or product positioning, marketing, and fulfillment, and we will help fill in the rest on how to use ChatGPT to do it even faster.

Experience the power of ChatGPT's AI-driven natural language processing tool that allows you to engage in conversations just like a human. Experience the power of ChatGPT's ultimate AI language model, which has been meticulously trained on vast amounts of data to deliver strikingly human-like responses. Whether seeking answers to complex queries or simply engaging in casual conversation, ChatGPT is the perfect companion that will rarely disappoint (I will talk about limitations in a later chapter).

Discover an incredible opportunity on ChatGPT with so many ways to make money online, including affiliate marketing! Promote your services and products through your blog or social media channels and earn commissions like never before. Elevate your earnings and effortlessly captivate your audience with the exceptional features of ChatGPT.

As I said, I have been making money online for years the hard way, with a lot of hard work and perseverance. With my expertise in guiding small and medium-sized companies to success, I can confidently affirm the significance of creative problem-solving and flexible thinking in today's dynamic business climate. No matter which routes you take, establishing a robust online presence and utilizing ChatGPT's tools and features is essential. With ChatGPT, making money online has always been challenging, and with my background, I can show you the way. While it takes time to establish yourself, ChatGPT provides you with the tools and resources you need to succeed. Discover the revolutionary ChatGPT, which is a groundbreaking advancement in artificial intelligence that has the potential to transform your financial future and ability to make even more money online faster than ever before. With a strong work ethic and unwavering determination, economic prosperity is attainable.

Dedication and hard work can turn this opportunity into a career, not just a way to make money online. Take advantage of the chance to achieve financial freedom from the comfort of your own home. Discover your ability to find the best strengths and unlock your potential to transform your passion into profit in the digital realm using ChatGPT to make money online.

With ChatGPT, this revolutionary Artificial Intelligence technology that generates human-like responses to text inputs effortlessly, and its unparalleled ability to mimic human communication, this cutting-edge technology is perfect for various applications. With the rapid advancement of technology, we can expect language models to become more sophisticated than ever. These models will be able to interact with humans more naturally, opening exciting new possibilities for communication, innovation, creativity, and making even more money.

Finish reading all my books, "How to Make Money with ChatGPT," to discover how to manifest even more financial success. ChatGPT, the leading chatbot platform that uses AI to offer personalized and engaging chats, is the best guide to making more money online. Chatbots are increasingly needed in the digital age. ChatGPT leads in reliable and cutting-edge solutions. ChatGPT improves sales, marketing, content creation, customer service, and more. The platform lets individuals, small enterprises, and giant corporations effortlessly design personalized chatbots for their purposes. This step-by-step book is the ultimate ChatGPT income guide. Discover new ways to earn today to advance in the digital age. Are you a successful internet entrepreneur looking to grow? Then ChatGPT is your ultimate goal-achieving tool. Discover the power of ChatGPT with this book and unlock new opportunities to grow your personal or business ventures while boosting your online earnings. ChatGPT empowers you to effortlessly engage with clients, streamline tedious duties, and craft unique content faster. Discover how ChatGPT can help you establish lucrative recurring revenue streams that generate income long after you've ceased actively promoting them. Customers today want quick, customized solutions, and successful people and companies are using chatbots powered by ChatGPT to address this demand. Chatbots enable 24/7 client service and reduce human-based customer service by interacting with clients anytime, anyplace. Chatbots optimize efficiency and cost by expediting operations and boosting productivity by handling repetitive requests.

As we witness the evolution of artificial intelligence and natural language processing, ChatGPT, its competitors, and other AI tools will likely assume a more significant role in our daily lives. Discover the impressive capabilities of ChatGPT while keeping in mind that, like any tool, it has its limitations.

Chatbots in e-commerce and digital marketing are available for new business prospects. ChatGPT lets businesses create custom conversation templates to attract customers, streamline sales, and personalize shopping experiences. Discover the ultimate guide to unlocking the potential of ChatGPT and earning more money online than ever before. This comprehensive book offers a systematic approach to implementing a proven strategy to transform your financial future. Discover the ultimate ChatGPT experience with expert tips, top-notch prompts for earning money, and clever techniques to maximize your ChatGPT journey. This book explores ChatGPT's financial potential. We will cover so many ways to make money, including but not limited to idea generation, content creation, freelancing, e-commerce, affiliate marketing, and so much more. But my real goal with this book is to give you the tools to act and use ChatGPT how you need it to make more money online this year.

Do you code, design, write, or want to be a virtual worker? Then ChatGPT can help you do all those faster and better. The platform is ideal for showcasing your skills and connecting with clients. ChatGPT can help freelancers, and so many others pursue their passions. Choose projects that interest you, maximize your potential, and access a more extensive customer base for repeat business.

Are you launching or improving your e-commerce store? ChatGPT can also help with that as well. ChatGPT is ready to support your entrepreneurial journey. ChatGPT streamlines order monitoring, management, and fulfillment for many entrepreneurs and organizations today. ChatGPT can help increase profits by letting you focus on your core business, if this is a side hustle or your full-time gig.

Do you create content today? You can easily make money with your excellent writing and love of connecting with readers. ChatGPT lets you promote products and earn commissions. Bloggers and social media influencers with a significant online presence prefer using ChatGPT for all the hard work on this strategy.

Chatbots are now essential to saving time with content creation, customer assistance, sales, and marketing. Use the right tools and ask the right question to succeed on the platform and make more money. Choose the best path, develop a solid online presence, and use chatbots to turn your hobbies into money. ChatGPT makes skill improvement and making more money fun!

If you see "PROMPT:" it is a suggestion of what you need to type. These are inputs and questions for ChatGPT. You will type this into the blank field at the bottom of chat.openai.com. Most will have a transparent "Send a message" notice. This book will have text that looks like this....

PROMPT: This is where you type this into ChatGPT using chat.openai.com

ChatGPT:

WHAT IS HERE WILL BE THE OUTPUT TEXT YOU SEE WHILE USING CHATGPT.

CHAPTER 1

ChatGPT and Its Potential for Online Income Generation

Join us on a journey through the intriguing history of ChatGPT in this chapter. Unveil the evolution of this powerful instrument and the various groundbreaking innovations that have propelled it to its current state. Discover the revolutionary technology behind ChatGPT and how it has revolutionized our interactions with machines. Uncover the myriad benefits of ChatGPT and how it has seamlessly integrated into our everyday routines. By this chapter's end, you'll comprehend ChatGPT and its potential to generate lucrative online revenue streams.

Discover the fascinating world of artificial intelligence (AI) and its evolution. While the concept of AI has been around since the 1950s, it was in the 2010s that AI language models truly captured the world's attention and became a ubiquitous tool in various industries. Meet IBM's Watson, the renowned language model that took the world by storm after winning against human champions on the quiz show "Jeopardy" in 2011. It's safe to say that Watson is a pioneer and a household name in language models and the precursor to what we have today.

Experience the next level of language models with OpenAI's

GPT (Generative Pretrained Transformer) series - the latest breakthrough in deep learning and neural networks. In 2018, GPT's first iteration was unveiled, shattering the boundaries of AI language models and showcasing their immense potential.

An AI-powered tool called ChatGPT was created by OpenAI, a company established in 2015 by a group of influential IT professionals, including Sam Altman and Elon Musk. The stated goal of OpenAI's AI research is to promote and build a friendly artificial intelligence environment. OpenAI is a nonprofit organization established in San Francisco in 2015 with a $1 billion pledge by Sam Altman, Elon Musk, Reid Hoffman, Peter Thiel, Jessica Livingston, and others.

ChatGPT's police release in 2020 has received updates that add even more sophisticated natural language processing features. Thanks to its capacity to learn from vast volumes of data, it is an effective tool for many businesses and has enormous potential for further growth.

ChatGPT's ability to comprehend context is one of its defining characteristics. GPT-1 could generate coherent and grammatically correct text after training on a large dataset. It can analyze input text and develop responses considering the larger conversation or topic.

ChatGPT can respond coherently and appropriately to user input because it has been trained on a vast corpus of text data. It has a high-level linguistic intelligence and can handle complex conversations with users.

The language model can respond to inquiries and help with tasks like emailing, writing essays, coding, etc. Although ChatGPT was primarily developed for research, many businesses and organizations now use it.

As a freelancer, ChatGPT can assist you in developing your style, coming up with fresh content ideas, and automating the editing process. Additionally, ChatGPT allows you to create chatbots that can provide round-the-clock customer service and support, freeing up your time for other money-making activities.

ChatGPT includes information from various research, books, and business magazines. ChatGPT unlocks pricing and customer behavior secrets. This book can help you maximize impact and profit with pricing. Finding the correct tools and technology in a world of information overload and competing demands can be challenging. Sifting through the noise and finding relevant information is the challenge.

To stay on topic and get back to why we are all here, reading the first book of the series, **How to Make Money Online**, I asked ChatGPT about the top ways to make money online.

PROMPT: give me the top 9 ways How to make money online

ChatGPT:

HERE ARE NINE INTERNET MONEY-MAKING OPPORTUNITIES:

1. FREELANCING ENTAILS PROVIDING YOUR EXPERTISE TO CUSTOMERS VIA AN ONLINE SERVICES MARKETPLACE LIKE UPWORK, FIVERR, OR FREELANCING.

2. GET PAID FOR YOUR THOUGHTS AND IDEAS BY TAKING ONLINE SURVEYS WITH COMPANIES LIKE SWAGBUCKS AND SURVEY JUNKIE.

3. WITH AFFILIATE MARKETING, YOU CAN RECEIVE A CUT OF THE PROFITS PRODUCED BY CUSTOMERS WHO CLICK ON YOUR SPECIAL REFERRAL LINK.

4. MAKE MONEY SHARING YOUR KNOWLEDGE BY TUTORING STUDENTS ONLINE THROUGH SITES LIKE CHEGG, TUTORME, AND VIPKID.

5. BY WORKING WITH A DROPSHIPPER, YOU CAN OPEN AN ONLINE BUSINESS WITHOUT THE NEED TO KEEP ANY STOCK ON HAND.

6. START A BLOG, AND FILL IT WITH ADVERTISING, SPONSORED MATERIAL, AND AFFILIATE LINKS.

7. WRITE BOOKS, MAKE MOVIES, OR SELL YOUR PHOTOGRAPHS ONLINE TO MAKE MONEY AS A CONTENT CREATOR.

8. **PRODUCE AND MARKET APPS FOR SMARTPHONES RUNNING THE ANDROID OR IOS OPERATING SYSTEMS.**

9. **ASSIST COMPANIES WITH THEIR SOCIAL MEDIA MANAGEMENT AND CONTENT DEVELOPMENT TO BOOST ENGAGEMENT AND SALES.**

KEEP IN MIND THAT YOU CAN'T EXPECT INSTANT RESULTS FROM ANY OF THESE STRATEGIES. IT'S ALSO CRUCIAL TO DO YOUR HOMEWORK AND PICK A STRATEGY THAT WORKS WELL WITH YOUR PERSONALITY AND HOBBIES.

After more detailed requests using tools discussed later in the book (better Prompts), I came up with several book ideas that make up the series *"**How to Make Money Online.**"* So yes, ChatGPT helped me and can also help you make money online.

ChatGPT is an asset for making money in various ways due to its ability to learn from vast amounts of data and produce human-like responses. Whether you're a content creator, freelancer, business owner, or entrepreneur, ChatGPT can simplify your income-generating endeavors and open fresh prospects for development.

Numerous types, iterations, and versions of ChatGPT can be used to make money, each with a unique size and set of features. We talked about the original ChatGPT 1 before, but here are some of their mothers and their primary distinctions:

GPT-2: This second-generation GPT model contains 1.5 billion parameters. It can produce high-quality text in a variety of designs and formats.

GPT-3: This model is the third iteration of the GPT family, and it can store up to 175 billion parameters. It can produce highly fluent and coherent text in various formats, such as essays, stories, and poems.

GPT-Neo: This open-source model created by EleutherAI includes up to 2.7 billion parameters. It is designed to be highly adaptable and flexible and can be taught to perform various tasks.

GPT-J: This is a scaled-up variant of GPT-3 developed by EleutherAI, with up to 6 billion parameters. It is one of the most significant available language models and can generate highly coherent and fluent text in various formats.

GShard, developed by Google, is a highly parallelized variant of the GPT model. It is designed to be highly scalable and can be trained using distributed computing on massive quantities of data.

The GPT-1 original model, which included 117 million parameters, was published in 2018. With 175 billion parameters, GPT-3 debuted in 2020 and is now one of the most significant and most potent language models accessible. It has been applied to various tasks, such as natural language processing, language translation, creative writing, and even music production.

Each model is designed for various use cases and applications, with benefits and drawbacks. Although larger models often demand more computational resources to train and use successfully, they are typically also more resilient and adaptive.

The ChatGPT prototype, made accessible on November 30, 2022, is built on the OpenAI GPT-3.5 and GPT 4. Since OpenAI uses GPT3.5, this can be a little confusing, and if you ever need more clarification, ask ChatGPT.

PROMPT: what model are you running

ChatGPT:

AS ONE OF THE MOST SOPHISTICATED LANGUAGE MODELS CURRENTLY ON THE MARKET, I WAS CREATED BY OPENAI AS A SIZABLE LANGUAGE MODEL BASED ON THE GPT-3 ARCHITECTURE. MY ARCHITECTURE AND CONFIGURATION, HOWEVER, MAY BE DIFFERENT FROM THOSE OF OTHER GPT-3 MODEL INSTANCES BECAUSE OPENAI HAS FURTHER ADJUSTED AND TAILORED ME FOR PARTICULAR USE CASES.

GPT-4 was released in March 2023 and is available in a limited format for paid premium subscribers. And depending on when you are reading this, there may be newer versions. Just ask ChatGPT if you need more information. ChatGPT continuously improves and diversifies, opening new avenues for generating revenue.

GPT-3.5 is what you get if you only sign up for the free version. If you pay or eventually use other tools, then GPT-4 will be the prominent language. GPT-4 is more innovative and team-oriented than previous models. It can generate, edit, and iterate when working with users on creative and technical writing activities like content creation, songwriting, screenwriting, or figuring out a user's writing style.

PROMPT: Explain the plot of little red riding hood in a sentence where each word must begin with the following letter in the alphabet from A to Z, without repeating any letters.

ChatGPT:

A BOLD, CURIOUS DAMSEL ENCOUNTERS A FEROCIOUS, GROWLING HUNTSMAN JUDICIOUSLY KEEPS LURKING MENACINGLY NEAR, OBSERVING PREDATORS QUIETLY, RUSHING SWIFTLY TOWARDS UNSUSPECTING VICTIMS, WANDERING, XENOPHOBIC YOUTH ZEALOUS.

There are several ways to increase business productivity as well using ChatGPT. With its sophisticated natural language processing abilities, various tasks and jobs can be automated, freeing up time and resources for other crucial endeavors. The following are a few possible applications for ChatGPT:

- ChatGPT can offer unique and practical material for websites, blogs, and social media. ChatGPT may generate a response customized to your needs and preferences by entering a prompt.

- ChatGPT can automate customer support, providing clients with around-the-clock assistance without involving humans. By doing so, you may respond more quickly and increase customer satisfaction.

- ChatGPT can manage emails, make appointments, and enter data. This can make time and resources available for more critical tasks. What task do you want to be automated?

- Text translation services provided by ChatGPT make it easier to communicate with persons from different linguistic and cultural backgrounds.

- ChatGPT may generate individualized recommendations for products, services, and information based on a user's tastes and behavior. The user experience can be improved, and as a result, engagement levels may increase.

- ChatGPT can assist teachers in developing innovative lesson plans, projects, assessments, and activities that follow predetermined learning objectives and curriculum requirements. Teachers can utilize ChatGPT to design and plan educational materials specific to each student's needs, such as presentations, worksheets, tests, and other instructional materials.

These are just a few examples, but I encourage you to make your list. I know we are very early in the book, but take the time to write down some use cases you can already see using ChatGPT to make your life easier and make even more money online.

ChatGPT, the most versatile and powerful tool, boosts productivity across individuals, industries, and applications. Social media managers can maximize a social media presence for an individual or a brand using ChatGPT as they invest in brand success and watch online engagement rise. ChatGPT makes creating social networking material accessible and can help schedule delivery. You may reach more potential clients with less money and in better time. ChatGPT platform can streamline content reuse, posting several places simultaneously, saving time.

Imagine impressing clients with the same high-quality work you've always done but faster than your competition. ChatGPT allows this and so much more. You can now see that this game-changing solution can boost your earnings.

ChatGPT lets you generate passive income long after your original investment. You can create fascinating eBooks and online courses to demonstrate and share your knowledge with more people. These valuable assets can be sold repeatedly after just one generation, making a consistent recurring income with no ongoing effort.

Marketing your product should maximize profitability and customer attractiveness. Finding balance takes time and effort. Finding the optimal equilibrium is problematic. Promoting your goods requires numerous considerations. Your product, target audience, channels, competition, and money are all factors. ChatGPT suggests using creative tools and procedures to automate mundane tasks so you can focus on what matters most.

CHAPTER 2

Setting Up and Understanding ChatGPT

Discover ChatGPT's many benefits and how it fits into our daily lives. If you haven't already, register **NOW** for ChatGPT. OpenAI is powerful, but only if you sign up today! Please follow these instructions: Visit https://openai.com/, click "product," and select "ChatGPT" from the drop-down. It's simple! Or go direct to Chat with OpenAI at https://chat.openai.com/.

Click the Sign-Up button in the top right corner to discover ChatGPT's power. Simply consenting to the terms of service and giving your name and email will unlock the platform's full potential. Secure your account with a strong password and email address. Click the OpenAI confirmation email link to confirm your email address. After signing up, you may easily log into your new account.

Again, there is a Free Version that uses 3.5, and it will be good for now and maybe all you ever need. The premium account is there to maximize GPT. "ChatGPT Plus" enhances ChatGPT! Exclusive privileges are available for just USD 20 a month. Get instant response and priority access to cutting-edge features.

Select the model upon login to maximize ChatGPT's potential. As a plus subscriber, you can choose from GPT-3, GPT-3.5, GPT-4, and more. Look at the top of the screen to verify which model you are using.

GPT-4 is the newest AI breakthrough. As a dedicated ChatGPT Plus user, you'll immediately notice a sleek contemporary feature at the top of your screen: a simple drop-down box with various cutting-edge models. ChatGPT Plus improves your chat experience. GPT-4 (or the latest stable version when reading) works best, but it's slower and has a 25-message-per-three-hour limit.

After creating your account, you can access sophisticated tools to improve workflow, boost productivity, and grow your business. To assist you in getting started and getting the most out of your ChatGPT account, OpenAI offers comprehensive documentation and tutorials.

By entering a prompt (a question or comment to which ChatGPT will respond) and hitting send, ChatGPT will produce an answer based on your prompt. To test how ChatGPT responds, try experimenting with different prompts and settings. For instance, you can experiment with other prompts to observe how they alter the text's inventiveness and randomness.

Begin with a simple "Hello," and you will get "Hello! How can I assist you today?"

PROMPT: Hello

ChatGPT:

"HELLO! HOW CAN I ASSIST YOU TODAY?"

Then play (practice) around, maybe like " Share five interesting facts about the moon." Or anything you are thinking about right now. Be creative; why are you reading this book? Ask ChatGPT to help. Here is what I asked, but what you ask is much more critical.

PROMPT: generate and share with me five facts about the moon

ChatGPT:

SURE, HERE ARE FIVE FASCINATING MOON-RELATED FACTS:

THE MOON IS THE LARGEST MOON RELATIVE TO ITS MOTHER PLANET, RANKING FIFTH IN SIZE IN THE SOLAR SYSTEM. IN ACTUALITY, THE MOON IS LARGER THAN EARTH BY MORE THAN A QUARTER.

IT IS ESTIMATED THAT THE MOON FORMED SOME 4.5 BILLION YEARS AGO, NOT LONG AFTER THE SOLAR SYSTEM AS A WHOLE. IT IS THOUGHT TO HAVE BEEN PRODUCED WHEN AN OBJECT THE SIZE OF MARS HIT WITH THE EARLY EARTH, LAUNCHING SPACE DEBRIS THAT LATER CAME TOGETHER TO FORM THE MOON.

THE MOON IS THE ONLY NATURALLY OCCURRING SATELLITE OF EARTH, AND IT IS ALSO THE ONLY PLACE IN THE SOLAR SYSTEM THAT HAS BEEN VISITED BY HUMANS. DURING THE APOLLO 11 MISSION IN 1969, NEIL ARMSTRONG AND EDWIN "BUZZ" ALDRIN WERE THE FIRST HUMANS TO SET FOOT ON THE MOON.

THE MOON'S SURFACE IS COVERED WITH CRATERS, MOUNTAINS, AND ENORMOUS, LEVEL PLAINS KNOWN AS MARIA. IT IS THOUGHT THAT

LONG-AGO VOLCANIC ACTIVITY PRODUCED THE MARIA BY SPEWING MOLTEN LAVA ONTO THE SURFACE AND FORMING BROAD, FLAT EXPANSES.

SINCE THE MOON ROTATES SYNCHRONOUSLY WITH EARTH, EARTH ALWAYS SEES THE SAME SIDE OF THE MOON. THIS IS DUE TO THE MOON'S ROTATIONAL PERIOD, WHICH IS EQUAL TO ITS ORBITAL PERIOD, WHICH IS THE LENGTH OF TIME IT TAKES TO ORBIT THE EARTH. SINCE WE CAN ONLY SEE ONE SIDE OF THE MOON, IT APPEARS TO BE STATIONARY IN THE SKY.

Keep asking questions, giving instructions, improving your prompts, or asking it to translate or analyze something. You may even ask it to make book recommendations or things you should be doing today. Please realize that this is an AI, and its communication is like an ongoing conversation. ChatGPT is an AI language model designed to understand and respond to your questions and requests using natural language processing. You can ask ChatGPT anything you like, and it will do its best to provide a helpful and informative response. Whether you need help with a specific task, want to learn something new, or want to chat. And yes, ChatGPT can keep you organized and even give helpful tips.

PROMPT: what should I be doing today?

ChatGPT:

I'M AN AI LANGUAGE MODEL, SO I NEED TO KNOW YOUR SPECIFIC PRIORITIES OR SCHEDULE, SO I CANNOT ADVISE YOU ON WHAT YOU SHOULD BE DOING RIGHT NOW. HOWEVER, THE FOLLOWING ARE SOME GENERAL POINTERS FOR MAXIMIZING YOUR DAY.

PLAN YOUR DAY OUT, INCLUDING ANY CRITICAL TASKS OR APPOINTMENTS YOU HAVE SCHEDULED BEFORE BEGIN. YOU'LL BE ABLE TO FOCUS BETTER AND WASTE LESS TIME AS A RESULT.

CHOOSE THE ITEMS ON YOUR TO-DO LIST THAT ARE MOST CRUCIAL TO FINISH FIRST. YOU'LL FEEL MORE PRODUCTIVE AS A RESULT AND WON'T BECOME OVERBURDENED LATER IN THE DAY.

BY GIVING YOUR BRAIN A CHANCE TO REST AND RECHARGE THROUGHOUT THE DAY, TAKING LITTLE BREAKS CAN INCREASE YOUR PRODUCTIVITY. THINK ABOUT GOING FOR A STROLL, STRETCHING, OR PERFORMING SOME BRIEF MEDITATION.

DRINK PLENTY OF WATER THROUGHOUT THE DAY TO STAY HYDRATED AND MAINTAIN YOUR FOCUS AND ALERTNESS.

SELF-CARE IS IMPORTANT. ALWAYS REMEMBER TO LOOK AFTER YOUR PHYSICAL AND EMOTIONAL HEALTH. THIS MIGHT ENTAIL GETTING ENOUGH REST, EATING WELL, AND ENGAGING IN ENJOYABLE ACTIVITIES.

IN THE END, PUTTING YOUR GOALS AND VALUES FIRST CAN HELP YOU MAKE THE BEST USE OF YOUR TIME AND ENERGY NOW.

Have fun....

PROMPT: is the moon real?

ChatGPT:

YES, THERE IS A MOON. IT IS A NATURAL SATELLITE OF THE EARTH AND IS SEEN AS A BRILLIANT OBJECT IN THE NIGHT SKY. SCIENTISTS HAVE DONE MUCH RESEARCH ON THE MOON, AND PEOPLE HAVE EVEN GONE THERE DURING THE APOLLO MISSIONS. SINCE ANCIENT TIMES, PEOPLE HAVE OBSERVED AND MEASURED THE MOON'S PRESENCE AND ITS IMPACTS ON EARTH, INCLUDING THE TIDES IT GENERATES AND THE

GRAVITATIONAL FORCE IT EXERTS. THEREFORE, THERE IS NO QUESTION THAT THE MOON IS A GENUINE SOLAR SYSTEM OBJECT.

Okay, maybe not too much fun; remember, we are here and need to keep the focus on how we can make more money online with ChatGPT. You will see a **Regenerate Response** button after you get a response. Feel free to click the button to verify that you will get different answers.

ChatGPT's user interface is created to be simple to use and intuitive, so users may quickly produce natural language responses to their cues. The prompt is where you enter the query, declaration, or another prompt you wish ChatGPT to address. This can be as straightforward as one word or as intricate as an entire paragraph or essay. Depending on the model and type of prompt, this may consist of text, graphics, or other media.

The history tab allows you to examine and keep track of all prior prompts and responses. By integrating ChatGPT with other programs and apps, developers can create unique solutions that utilize ChatGPT's natural language processing capabilities.

Several platforms and programs have integrated with the OpenAI API and can access ChatGPT. With development experience, you can incorporate the OpenAI API into your applications using the available programming libraries and documentation. This would allow you to construct custom solutions that leverage ChatGPT's capabilities.

ChatGPT's user interface is created to be straightforward and approachable while offering solid and sophisticated natural language processing capabilities. Users can fully utilize

ChatGPT's capabilities and obtain exceptional results using appropriate strategies and procedures. Here are some pointers on how to get the most out of ChatGPT. ChatGPT provides a range of models with various features and degrees of complexity. Spend time experimenting with several models to locate the one that best suits your unique needs and demands.

ChatGPT's settings can be changed. Find the most effective settings for your use case by experimenting with parameters like response length, temperature, and top-p. The input prompt's precision and clarity significantly impact the quality of the generated response. Give ChatGPT precise information to produce an accurate and helpful answer by providing precise and explicit suggestions. Ensure the generated responses are correct, logical, and appropriate for your needs.

Consider integrating ChatGPT with other programs and devices or combining it with human wisdom and intuition. By highlighting these pointers and tricks, users can fully utilize ChatGPT and accomplish excellent outcomes in various applications and sectors. With some testing and experience, ChatGPT can be an invaluable tool for increasing productivity, creating original and exciting content, and attaining outstanding results.

Once you've determined what to ask, carefully word your prompt to communicate precisely what you want ChatGPT to respond to. Include any pertinent details or context that will assist ChatGPT in generating a more accurate response. After entering your question, some chatbot interfaces require you to select a "send" or "submit" button, while others generate a response automatically. Try this out; ask your question to

ChatGPT. Did you get the answer you expected? It took me months of learning Prompts to get the desired results, so this will take practice.

After entering your question, ChatGPT will construct a response based on your input. It is essential to evaluate the response to ensure accuracy and relevance thoroughly. You can ask follow-up questions or reword your prompt to elicit a more precise response. If the reaction generated by ChatGPT is unsatisfactory or does not fully answer your query, try entering a different prompt or rephrasing your original prompt. The desired response may require multiple attempts, but ChatGPT is designed to learn from its interactions and generate increasingly accurate reactions over time. Provide as much pertinent information as feasible if your question or request pertains to a particular subject or circumstance.

ChatGPT has been trained in proper English, so adequate grammar and spelling will help it better comprehend your input. As a language model, ChatGPT may require some time to evaluate your information and generate a response. It is essential to be patient and wait for the model's response. ChatGPT is trained on vast data, and alternative wording can sometimes produce a better result.

Although ChatGPT can generate responses on various subjects, it is best to remain on topic and avoid moving from one issue to another. ChatGPT is intended to be a valuable and informative resource, so please avoid using inappropriate or offensive language.

ChatGPT is a conversational AI model so customer service might be the best use case. ChatGPT is a multi-prompt, context-sensitive bot with access to the previous prompts' context, making it the perfect choice for customer responses. Like most chatbots, he claims the first inquiry needs to be recovered or forgotten when you ask the second.

The translation is also a great use case because it effectively contextualizes and discusses. Suppose I speak English, and you want to hear the conversation in Spanish. In that case, the translation engine will appear, but because it is conversational AI, it will sound like a human, and the translation need not be limited to text; voice translation is another option.

The documentation use case is another usable situation for AI. It is good at producing legal documents based on certain responses you expect. It can review published rules and laws and generate legal memos and briefs.

CHAPTER 3

Maximizing Productivity with ChatGPT to Earn Online Income

Maximize your productivity and earn money online effortlessly with ChatGPT. Make sure you go back to Chapter 2 and set it up if you still need to. And spend some more time with practice prompts relevant to why you are reading this book and get familiar with the platform to start reaping its benefits. In this chapter, discover many techniques to amplify your productivity and boost your earnings with ChatGPT.

Streamline your business or online activities with ChatGPT's automation capabilities. From customer service to scheduling and email management, ChatGPT has got you covered. Let ChatGPT take care of these activities effortlessly, freeing up your valuable time to focus on other crucial aspects of your business.

ChatGPT's primary objective is to provide individuals, organizations, and developers with a robust and flexible conversational AI and NLP platform to help them build more captivating and interactive tools and applications. Unlock the full potential with rich language capabilities, allowing you to create complex and sophisticated designs like never before.

With its uncanny ability to provide human-like responses to a wide range of inquiries and prompts, ChatGPT is an invaluable tool for chatbots, personal assistants, customer service, and other conversational AI applications. The advanced capabilities include machine translation, language comprehension, and text classification. With its impressive features, this tool can handle various natural language processing tasks, making it an invaluable asset across multiple fields and applications. The continuous development of this area will bring immense benefits to you.

Like any other AI system, algorithmic bias, privacy concerns, and responsible usage are important factors. OpenAI addresses these concerns and ensures that ChatGPT is utilized respectably and conscientiously. ChatGPT strives to deliver a powerful and flexible solution for NLP and AI, elevate the realm of NLP and AI exploration, and tackle any partiality and ethical concerns associated with its implementation.

You can get inspiration from ChatGPT for blog pieces, social media updates, and even eBooks. Additionally, you can utilize ChatGPT to build chatbots that converse with your consumers, respond to their inquiries, and lead them through your sales funnel.

ChatGPT can also help you identify patterns and trends in your sector, giving you the advantage of staying current and making wise business decisions. You can boost productivity, simplify workflow, and ultimately earn even more money online by utilizing ChatGPT's features.

A strong tool like ChatGPT can boost productivity and generate more cash online. Users may create high-quality material, automate repetitive operations, and improve efficiency using the tool's natural language processing features. ChatGPT can produce material for blogs, social media, and other online venues, resulting in recurring passive income streams.

ChatGPT can automate data entry and analysis, streamline support operations, and offer intelligent support for various applications and industries. ChatGPT may be an excellent ally for boosting productivity and generating online money with the correct approaches, prompts, and methods.

You can even ask ChatGPT for suggestions on increasing your online income. What if you didn't know anything about AI and wanted ChatGPT to help you find ways to make money? You can see that ChatGPT will provide you with ideas for online courses, product sales, video production, freelancing, email marketing, blogging, and self-publishing. What did you ask ChatGPT today? Nothing, go back to the application and ask how you can make more money, be specific.

You can get help from ChatGPT to create excellent content for your company, such as blog pieces, social media updates, and product descriptions. Doing this can ensure the content is pertinent and interesting while saving time and money.

PROMPT: generate eight ways to earn money for an entrepreneur in {TOPIC}. What response did you get? Anything that you can act on today? If not, ask in more detail. ChatGPT can be used to generate business ideas. Get personalized side business suggestions that suit your preferences. By learning about your interests, skills, and challenges, ChatGPT will work its magic to produce customized company concepts that meet your needs.

PROMPT: I am interested in technology, fishing, and cooking; how can I earn money online

ChatGPT:

YOU CAN MAKE MONEY ONLINE IN A VARIETY OF WAYS DEPENDING ON YOUR INTERESTS IN TECHNOLOGY, FISHING, AND CUISINE. HERE ARE A FEW CONCEPTS:

START A TECHNOLOGY BLOG TO SHARE YOUR EXPERTISE AND IDEAS WITH OTHERS IF YOU ARE INTERESTED IN TECHNOLOGY. RUNNING ADVERTISEMENTS, SPONSORED CONTENT, OR AFFILIATE MARKETING ARE ALL WAYS TO MAKE MONEY FROM YOUR SITE.

SELL FISHING EQUIPMENT ONLINE: YOU CAN OPEN AN ONLINE SHOP OFFERING FISHING SUPPLIES. YOU CAN PURCHASE GOODS FROM DROPSHIPPERS OR WHOLESALERS AND PROMOTE YOUR STORE VIA PAID SOCIAL MEDIA ADVERTISING.

CREATE A BLOG OR YOUTUBE CHANNEL FOR YOUR FISHING CONTENT IF YOU'RE PASSIONATE ABOUT IT. YOU CAN SHARE YOUR FISHING EXPLOITS, ADVICE, AND TRICKS ON YOUR BLOG OR CHANNEL. ADS AND SPONSORSHIPS ARE TWO WAYS YOU CAN EARN MONEY FROM YOUR CONTENT.

SELL YOUR OWN COOKING OR FISHING LURES ONLINE: IF YOU HAVE A KNACK FOR CREATING YOUR OWN CULINARY OR FISHING LURES, YOU CAN SELL THEM ONLINE THROUGH YOUR OWN WEBSITE OR ONLINE MARKETPLACES LIKE ETSY OR AMAZON.

CREATE A COOKING BLOG OR YOUTUBE CHANNEL TO SHARE RECIPES AND COOKING ADVICE: IF YOU ENJOY COOKING, YOU CAN DO SO. ADS AND SPONSORSHIPS ARE TWO WAYS YOU CAN EARN MONEY FROM YOUR CONTENT.

BECOME A FOOD OR TECHNOLOGY WRITER BY PENNING ARTICLES OR REVIEWS FOR WEBSITES THAT FOCUS ON THESE TOPICS. EDITORS ARE

OPEN TO YOUR IDEAS, AND YOU CAN EVEN WRITE FOR CONTENT FARMS LIKE UPWORK OR FIVERR.

DESIGN AN APP: YOU CAN DESIGN YOUR OWN CULINARY OR FISHING APP AND MAKE MONEY THROUGH IN-APP PURCHASES OR ADVERTS IF YOU ARE SKILLED AT PROGRAMMING OR APP DEVELOPMENT.

TEACH ONLINE COURSES: ON WEBSITES LIKE UDEMY OR COURSERA, YOU CAN DESIGN AND SELL ONLINE COURSES IF YOU ARE AN EXPERT IN ANY OF YOUR INTERESTS.

The Above was done with the ChatGPT 3.5 model. Below is the response using ChatGPT 4. Make sure you know which one you are using. Look at the top of the screen.

ChatGPT:

SURE, GIVEN YOUR INTERESTS IN TECHNOLOGY, FISHING, AND COOKING, THERE ARE A MULTITUDE OF WAYS THAT YOU COULD EARN MONEY ONLINE. A FEW SUGGESTIONS:

1. CONTENT CREATION: YOU CAN START A BLOG OR A YOUTUBE CHANNEL SHARING YOUR KNOWLEDGE AND EXPERIENCES ABOUT TECHNOLOGY, FISHING, AND COOKING. THIS COULD INCLUDE PRODUCT REVIEWS, TUTORIALS, TIPS, AND TRICKS, OR GENERAL ADVICE. AS YOUR FOLLOWING GROWS, YOU CAN MONETIZE THROUGH ADS, SPONSORSHIPS, AND AFFILIATE MARKETING.

2. E-COMMERCE: YOU CAN SELL FISHING EQUIPMENT OR TECH GADGETS ONLINE. IF YOU'RE INTO COOKING, YOU CAN ALSO SELL HOMEMADE FOOD PRODUCTS OR COOKING SUPPLIES. WEBSITES LIKE ETSY, EBAY, OR EVEN SETTING UP YOUR OWN SHOPIFY STORE COULD BE GREAT PLATFORMS FOR THIS.

3. ONLINE COURSES OR WEBINARS: IF YOU'RE AN EXPERT IN ANY OF YOUR INTEREST AREAS, CONSIDER TEACHING OTHERS BY

CREATING AN ONLINE COURSE OR HOSTING WEBINARS. WEBSITES LIKE UDEMY, TEACHABLE, OR SKILLSHARE ARE PERFECT PLATFORMS FOR THIS.

4. AFFILIATE MARKETING: IF YOU HAVE A STRONG SOCIAL MEDIA PRESENCE OR A BLOG, YOU CAN EARN MONEY BY PROMOTING OTHER PEOPLE'S PRODUCTS. AMAZON HAS A GREAT AFFILIATE PROGRAM, AS DO MANY TECH, COOKING, AND FISHING COMPANIES.

5. WRITING E-BOOKS: IF YOU'RE A GOOD WRITER, YOU CAN WRITE AND SELL EBOOKS ABOUT TECHNOLOGY, FISHING, AND COOKING ON AMAZON OR OTHER ONLINE PLATFORMS.

6. APP DEVELOPMENT: IF YOU HAVE TECHNICAL SKILLS, YOU COULD DEVELOP AN APP RELATED TO FISHING OR COOKING. FOR EXAMPLE, AN APP THAT PROVIDES COOKING RECIPES OR AN APP THAT GIVES FISHING TIPS AND TRACKS THE BEST FISHING SPOTS.

7. FREELANCING: YOU CAN OFFER YOUR SKILLS IN TECHNOLOGY, LIKE WEB DESIGN, PROGRAMMING, TECH SUPPORT, ETC., ON PLATFORMS LIKE UPWORK OR FIVERR.

8. VIRTUAL COOKING CLASSES: WITH THE RISE OF REMOTE LEARNING, YOU CAN OFFER VIRTUAL COOKING CLASSES THROUGH ZOOM OR ANOTHER VIDEO CONFERENCING TOOL.

9. PAID ONLINE SURVEYS/REVIEWS: COMPANIES ARE ALWAYS LOOKING FOR CONSUMER OPINIONS ON THEIR PRODUCTS. GIVEN YOUR INTERESTS, YOU MIGHT FIND OPPORTUNITIES TO BE PAID FOR REVIEWING TECH GADGETS, FISHING GEAR, OR COOKING TOOLS.

10. PHOTOGRAPHY: IF YOU HAVE SKILLS IN PHOTOGRAPHY, YOU COULD SELL PICTURES OF YOUR COOKING CREATIONS OR YOUR FISHING TRIPS ON STOCK PHOTOGRAPHY WEBSITES LIKE SHUTTERSTOCK OR ISTOCKPHOTO.

IT'S IMPORTANT TO REMEMBER THAT MANY OF THESE OPTIONS WILL TAKE TIME TO BUILD UP A CLIENT BASE OR FOLLOWING, BUT WITH CONSISTENCY AND QUALITY CONTENT OR SERVICES, THEY CAN BE PROFITABLE. ALSO, REMEMBER TO CONSIDER ANY LEGAL OR TAX IMPLICATIONS OF STARTING AN ONLINE BUSINESS.

It'll display ChatGPT responses for a few prompt instances to demonstrate how much the output can vary based on your questions. But I will also show you the PROMPTS sometimes so you will get used to typing the prompt and seeing the response yourself.

How ChatGPT Can Assist Influencers Generate Income

ChatGPT can help influencers earn money in various ways by enabling them to create personalized content, interact with their followers, and monetize their platforms. Influencers can utilize the following strategies to benefit from ChatGPT.

Are you an influencer? Or want to be one? Have you written blog posts or social media content? What to be able to do it faster with better results? Then practice.

ChatGPT can produce personalized content, such as blog posts, social media updates, and videos, tailored to each follower's interests and preferences. This can help influencers create engaging content that resonates with their audience and generates more views, engagement, and revenue.

How to automate tedious jobs with ChatGPT to free up time for income-generating activities

One of the main advantages of adopting ChatGPT is its capacity to automate time-consuming and laborious operations, freeing up vital time for activities that generate cash. Users may automate data entry, content development, and customer service with ChatGPT, freeing them up to concentrate on more strategically important and high-value jobs.

Before automating repetitive and time-consuming processes with ChatGPT, users should identify them. Then, users can create prompts that provide the data ChatGPT needs to provide accurate and helpful responses. After establishing these inquiries, ChatGPT can be set up to produce answers automatically, freeing users to focus on other tasks.

If a user administers a blog, for example, they may use ChatGPT to automate content creation by providing ideas that result in high-quality postings, saving valuable time and effort. In this manner, ChatGPT can automate routine inquiries, streamlining customer service procedures and freeing up support staff to focus on more challenging issues.

Have you written a blog for some time? Try to copy and paste some of them in ChatGPT and ask it to expand your blog to 500 words. Do you like the content? Then change the prompt. There are prompts at the end of this book, and there is a book of 3,000 more I can send you; click the link at the beginning for the prompts.

ChatGPT can suggest affiliate programs for you to join and can assist you in identifying goods and services that are likely to appeal to your target market. You can get paid a commission on any sales made using your platform by recommending these goods or services to your followers. Ask ChatGPT to give you a list of programs in your {NICHE}.

Using ChatGPT to automate time-consuming operations, users can boost productivity and efficiency while freeing up valuable time for activities that provide income. ChatGPT can be useful for automating repetitive tasks and generating top-notch results without much originality or ingenuity.

The role of ChatGPT in assisting data collection and research for financial gain

ChatGPT can help with data collection and research, which can be used to earn money. By employing the tool's natural language processing capabilities, users may easily and quickly access data on various topics, from market trends and customer preferences to competitive intelligence and industry insights.

This information can generate new products or services, enhance marketing strategies, and make business decisions. Thanks to ChatGPT's ability to analyze massive amounts of data quickly and reliably, users may save time and effort while gaining essential insights that can help them stay ahead of the competition.

Whether users are gathering consumer feedback, monitoring social media trends, or conducting market research, ChatGPT can be a helpful tool for information gathering and research, supporting users in making more informed decisions and efficiently producing cash.

Numerous corporate processes like appointment scheduling and inventory management can be automated using ChatGPT. By reducing the time and effort needed to handle these procedures, you can boost efficiency and production and focus on crucial company operations. Your organization can benefit from ChatGPT's enhanced customer engagement and happiness, more sales and leads, product and service optimization, and increased productivity. By utilizing ChatGPT's insights and skills, you may fortify your company and achieve long-term growth. Using ChatGPT may be a fantastic tool for creating ideas and material.

You can use ChatGPT, for instance, to create personalized to-do lists based on your priorities and due dates. It can also help you schedule your tasks and appointments more effectively by considering factors like your energy levels and natural rhythms.

You can use ChatGPT to manage your emails, send and receive messages, and write papers and reports. It can also help you conduct research and amass knowledge more effectively by summarizing articles, giving insights, and providing essential details.

Using ChatGPT to manage your time and productivity, you can devote more valuable time to income-generating activities. Whether you're a freelancer, business owner, or employee, increasing your productivity can help you earn more money, advance your profession, and achieve your objectives. Why not try ChatGPT and see how it can increase your output and earnings?

Enhancing earning potential by using ChatGPT for brainstorming and idea generation

Your thought and idea-generation capacity might increase your chances of earning more money with ChatGPT. Using ChatGPT's capabilities, users can provide open-ended queries or prompts to generate various ideas, from economic prospects to artistic projects. ChatGPT can help users improve and develop their ideas by providing information, feedback, and insights. By using ChatGPT for idea generation and brainstorming, people can release their creative potential and find new sources of income, enhancing their financial abundance and expanding their opportunities for advancement.

ChatGPT can be a useful tool for enhancing SEO and boosting website traffic by assisting users in creating unique and worthwhile content. Using ChatGPT to produce content ideas that align with your target audience's interests and are in line with your business objectives is one way to achieve this. You can use ChatGPT to develop content that speaks to the wants and interests of your audience by employing keywords and phrases that are most significant to them. This will increase the likelihood that your website will rank high in the relevant search results and keep your audience engaged.

Refining and optimizing already-written material is another way to use ChatGPT for content development. ChatGPT can assist users in identifying areas for improvement in their current material, such as adding more detail or incorporating more pertinent keywords by posing questions or suggestions linked to themes or keywords.

ChatGPT can also produce educational and interesting content for articles, blogs, and social media updates. You can produce well-written, well-structured material suited to your audience by utilizing ChatGPT's natural language processing capabilities. This can assist in boosting interest and website traffic, ultimately resulting in better SEO and more sales.

Be specific in your requests and establish a clear purpose. It will take some practice, but this is perhaps the most crucial thing you need to master to guarantee that your responses from ChatGPT are exactly what you want. As you may recall, a "Prompt" is what ChatGPT refers to when you ask it a question. As an illustration, you want to help create a marketing tagline for your digital marketing company.

PROMPT: provide an example of how to write a marketing tagline

ChatGPT:

OF COURSE, THIS IS AN ILLUSTRATION OF A MARKETING SLOGAN FOR A BUSINESS ENGAGED IN DIGITAL MARKETING:

"UNLEASH THE FULL POTENTIAL OF YOUR COMPANY WITH [COMPANY NAME]: YOUR PARTNER IN SUCCESSFUL DIGITAL MARKETING"

THIS TAGLINE COMBINES THE FIRM NAME AND ITS VALUE PROPOSITION ("YOUR PARTNER IN DIGITAL MARKETING SUCCESS") WITH A CALL TO ACTION ("UNLEASH YOUR BUSINESS'S FULL POTENTIAL"). IT CONVEYS A SENSE OF COOPERATION AND PARTNERSHIP, IMPLYING THAT THE BUSINESS IS DEDICATED TO COLLABORATING CLOSELY WITH ITS CLIENTS TO MEET THEIR MARKETING OBJECTIVES. IT ALSO SUGGESTS THAT THE FIRM HAS THE KNOWLEDGE AND RESOURCES NECESSARY TO SUPPORT ENTERPRISES IN THRIVING IN THE DIGITAL SPHERE.

Selling and marketing professionals can benefit from ChatGPT by optimizing the client personalization they can offer through the content they deliver. For this reason, this AI can be used in the following ways across channels, including marketing initiatives, commercials, and social media platforms. Keyword

Analysis involves ChatGPT assessing sizable blocks of text material people provide and returning a verbiage analysis that includes the most popular terms. What these copies lack, however, is personality and verve, which may be added to the copies with minimal human interaction.

Collecting and complaint redressal can be automated by integrating an intelligent chatbot, like ChatGPT, into a product-focused website or application. It may also be used for A/B testing by instructing the AI to produce two versions of the product description and receiving insightful data on the campaign's effectiveness from several focus groups.

PROMPT: What type of business can a data analyst with skills in digital marketing pursue to make $1,000 per day with a modest investment and only 10 hours per week of work?

ChatGPT:

I just showed you the prompt above. Hopefully, you typed it into your own and now see the response for yourself. And again, make the prompt your question to make this even more relevant. Now, let's drill down a little from the above request.

PROMPT: now tell me about a great but less well-known online business opportunity.

ChatGPT:

THERE ARE SEVERAL EXCITING BUT NOT AS WELL-KNOWN WAYS TO GENERATE MONEY ONLINE:

SOME WEBSITES PAY USERS TO SERVE AS ONLINE JURORS. THESE PEOPLE OFFER INPUT TO ATTORNEYS AND LEGAL FIRMS ON MOCK

TRIALS, ENABLING THEM TO GATHER INSIGHTFUL INFORMATION BEFORE TO COURT.

INTERIOR DESIGNER SOFTWARE AND A CREATIVE EYE ARE ALL YOU NEED TO START YOUR CAREER AS A VIRTUAL INTERIOR DESIGNER. A BESPOKE DESIGN PLAN AND 3D RENDERINGS ARE PRODUCED BY THE DESIGNER WHEN CLIENTS UPLOAD IMAGES OF THEIR HOME OR WORKPLACE AREA.

MANAGER OF SOCIAL MEDIA FOR SMALL BUSINESSES: EVEN IF THEY CAN'T AFFORD TO HIRE A FULL-TIME STAFF, SMALL BUSINESSES FREQUENTLY NEED ASSISTANCE MANAGING THEIR SOCIAL MEDIA ACCOUNTS. THROUGH FOCUSED ADVERTISING AND CONTENT PRODUCTION, YOU MAY ASSIST BUSINESSES IN INCREASING THEIR ONLINE PRESENCE AND GENERATING LEADS AS A FREELANCE SOCIAL MEDIA MANAGER.

ONLINE TUTORS ARE HIGHLY SOUGHT AFTER BECAUSE OF THE POPULARITY OF ONLINE LEARNING AND THEIR ABILITY TO INSTRUCT STUDENTS IN MATH, SCIENCE, AND FOREIGN LANGUAGES. THROUGH ONLINE SERVICES LIKE SKYPE OR ZOOM, YOU MAY TUTOR STUDENTS FROM ALL AROUND THE WORLD.

TRANSCRIBER: TRANSCRIBERS ARE THOSE WHO LISTEN TO AUDIO RECORDINGS AND TURN THEM INTO WRITTEN DOCUMENTATION. FOR THOSE WHO ARE METICULOUS AND HAVE STRONG TYPING SKILLS, THIS POSITION IS APPROPRIATE.

OVERALL, ASIDE FROM THE MORE CONVENTIONAL POSSIBILITIES, THERE ARE A TON OF UNIQUE METHODS TO GENERATE MONEY ONLINE. THE SECRET IS TO CHOOSE A MARKET SEGMENT ABOUT WHICH YOU ARE ENTHUSIASTIC AND TO USE YOUR EXPERTISE TO BUILD A SUCCESSFUL INTERNET BUSINESS.

Even though the list is wholly different, to even further drill down with more details, I typed:

PROMPT: What if I want to make even more money with less time spent each week?

ChatGPT:

After the response, it also said… Remember that earning money frequently takes time, risk, and effort. It is finding the right balance between earning money and preserving a positive work-life balance.

The answers can, and did, change drastically depending on how the prompt was phrased, and it has become increasingly aware of my preferences with each successive prompt. Telling it I wanted to make even more money caused the entire list to shift rather than just the ideas themselves.

If I had included "I like food and cars" after or in addition to the initial prompt, the outcomes would have been different. Also, it was understood that we were still discussing the same concept, making money online, each time, and I didn't have to rephrase the prompt completely.

Don't hesitate to practice experimenting with various prompts and verbiage in your questions. You might discover a brand-new method for producing content you had never considered before. You can instruct it to help even more with content creation by adding things to your prompts like "Write this in a witty, funny, engaging tone" or even "Write this in the style of a specific person," as I did in the introduction using was William Shakespeare style.

What if you ask ChatGPT to develop imaginative and compelling stories that can hold readers' attention for extended periods? And ask it to compose a story that takes place in the future. Please DO NOT copy and paste the results into a blog or book, as authorities can and will be able to see that an AI wrote it. But why not use ChatGPT to help with the title, the outline, the summary, and even help generate ideas to help get you started?

If you receive a response from ChatGPT but are still looking for more satisfaction, you can always ask it again differently or follow up with a more detailed question.

PROMPT: Act as Albert Einstein and create a tweet about how to make money online

ChatGPT:

"UNDERSTANDING THE DYNAMICS OF THE ONLINE WORLD IS MUCH LIKE UNDERSTANDING THE COSMOS. #1: COMPREHEND THE LAWS – IN THIS CASE, KNOW YOUR MARKET. #2: IDENTIFY YOUR SPACE – YOUR NICHE. #3: WORK DILIGENTLY AND PERSISTENTLY, FOR THE UNIVERSE REWARDS CONSISTENT ENERGY. #MAKEMONEYONLINE"

Additionally, you'll learn that you may respond differently to the same query. You may instruct ChatGPT to generate multiple responses simultaneously, which is helpful if you need to select something like email subject lines or titles for videos or blogs because you can't immediately think of one that strikes a chord with you.

Even pre-existing content can be entered into ChatGPT, which will respond when you ask for suggestions on improving your previous prompt or content. Then, you can focus on elements like tone, readability, and clarity. You can ask ChatGPT to share suggestions on making this email easier to read and more professional. By considering these suggestions and using trial and error, you can make the most of ChatGPT to create content that resonates with your audience and advances your goals.

PROMPT: Use the making money idea above. Identify the needs and wants of people that still need to be fulfilled, and use your imagination to create innovative solutions. Feel free to take risks and produce 100 words for a blog.

ChatGPT:

IN THIS VAST EXPANSE OF THE DIGITAL UNIVERSE, UNMET NEEDS AND DESIRES ARE LIKE UNDISCOVERED STARS, READY TO BE ILLUMINATED BY YOUR UNIQUE IDEAS. HARNESS YOUR IMAGINATION TO SCULPT INNOVATIVE SOLUTIONS THAT RESONATE WITH THESE NEEDS. UNDERSTAND THAT THE PATH TO TRUE INNOVATION IS OFTEN PAVED WITH RISKS. FEAR NOT, FOR THESE ARE BUT STEPPING STONES TO GREATNESS. IF YOUR SOLUTION MEETS A GENUINE NEED, IT WILL CREATE ITS OWN DEMAND, MUCH LIKE A COMET CARVING ITS OWN PATH. THIS AUDACIOUS BLEND OF CREATIVITY, RISK-TAKING, AND DISCERNMENT COULD BE YOUR BLUEPRINT TO MAKING MONEY ONLINE, SHINING BRIGHT IN THE DIGITAL COSMOS.

Even though ChatGPT can deliver excellent results, it is crucial to remember that it cannot replace human editing. While ChatGPT can speed up material development and save time, more is needed than a human editor's skilled judgment and imagination.

It is advised to carefully analyze the generated text after utilizing ChatGPT. This includes proofreading the content to ensure that it adheres to your standards, checking for grammatical and spelling issues, and making that the tone and voice are consistent with your brand or message.

Furthermore, even though ChatGPT is a very effective tool for creating content, it is important to remember that it must maintain the importance of human editing. Review and edit the generated text to ensure it adheres to your standards and accurately conveys your brand's message.

CHAPTER 4

Key Techniques for ChatGPT Users

Unlock the full potential of your content creation with ChatGPT. While already a powerful tool, there are advanced techniques you can utilize to take your content to the next level.

To ensure optimal results from ChatGPT, providing comprehensive prompts containing all necessary information is crucial. Provide ChatGPT with all the necessary information, including the desired tone, style, target audience, and other relevant details to help you understand your requirements.

Experience the full range of creativity with ChatGPT's temperature setting, which allows you to adjust the level of inventiveness and surprise in the generated text. By default, this parameter is set to 0.7. However, depending on your specific needs, you can adjust it to a higher or lower value. Experience the unexpected and creative power of language written at a higher temperature while enjoying the predictability and security of language written at a lower temperature. Have you changed this setting to see the results for yourself? Please do it now.

Take control of your generated text with ChatGPT's length setting. Adjust the amount of text generated for each query to your liking. Customize the parameter setting to your liking by adjusting it to a higher or lower value as needed, although the default is 2048 characters. Customize the length option to suit your needs, whether you require text for a specific prompt. Have you asked it to shorten or expand on any output yet?

Customize the level of unpredictability in your generated text with ChatGPT's top-p setting adjustment feature. Set to 1 by default, this parameter can be easily adjusted to fit your specific needs, whether you require a higher or lower value. Achieve greater text predictability with a lower top-p value or opt for a higher top-p setting to generate more unpredictable text.

ChatGPT is a valuable tool, but it should differ from the human touch of editing. Take the time to meticulously edit the result to guarantee a flawless outcome that exceeds your expectations.

It is possible to use ChatGPT in a few ways to boost productivity, improve efficiency, and make money online. ChatGPT enables users to engage in more intricate interactions with the system by enabling the creation of multi-turn discussions. This may be helpful in situations involving customer service or sales, where customers may be required to give more specific information or ask several questions.

One of the most powerful tools is to use other systems or processes you can use by yourself; use ChatGPT to speed up the process. And depending on how you learn, the Pareto Principle may be the best-advanced technique you can use. According to the Pareto Principle, commonly called the 80/20 rule, roughly 80% of outcomes result from 20% of causes. In other words, a small number of inputs or efforts typically result in many outcomes.

This idea is named after the Italian economist Vilfredo Pareto, who noted that only 20% of the people in Italy held 80% of the country's land. Since then, numerous disciplines, including business, economics, and individual productivity, have used the Pareto Principle.

For instance, according to the Pareto Principle, just 20% of a company's consumers or products account for 80% of its income. A corporation

might enhance areas already functioning well to have the biggest impact.The Pareto Principle may also suggest that only 20% of a person's chores or habits account for 80% of their performance in terms of personal productivity. One prompt would be "transform key concepts or lessons from {TOPIC} into engaging stories to help me better understand the material."

PROMPT: transform key concepts or lessons from {how to make money online} into engaging stories to help me better understand the material

ChatGPT:

SURE, LET ME SHARE A FEW EXAMPLES WITH YOU TO ASSIST YOU GRASP THE FUNDAMENTAL IDEAS AND TEACHINGS OF EARNING MONEY ONLINE:

NARROW YOUR FOCUS TO STAND OUT: ONCE UPON A TIME, A WOMAN BY THE NAME OF MARIA HAD A PASSION FOR MAKING HANDCRAFTED SOAP. SHE MADE AN ATTEMPT TO SELL THEM ONLINE, BUT SHE RECEIVED LITTLE INTEREST. MARIA MADE THE DECISION TO FOCUS HER BUSINESS ON PRODUCING VEGAN SOAPS FOR THOSE WITH SENSITIVE SKIN ONE DAY. SHE CONCENTRATED ON THIS MARKET AND DEVELOPED A DISTINCTIVE BRAND THAT SET HER APART FROM OTHER SOAP

PRODUCERS. SHE EVEN DEVELOPED SOCIAL MEDIA POSTS AND BLOG ENTRIES EXCLUSIVELY FOR PERSONS WITH SENSITIVE SKIN. MARIA'S BUSINESS SOON TOOK OFF, AND SHE WAS EARNING A SIZABLE SUM OF MONEY FROM THE SALE OF HER VEGAN SOAPS.

THE TAKEAWAY IS THAT YOU MAY DIFFERENTIATE YOURSELF FROM THE COMPETITION AND DRAW IN A DEVOTED CLIENTELE WHO WILL PAY FOR YOUR GOODS OR SERVICES BY NARROWING DOWN AND SPECIALIZING IN A PARTICULAR SECTOR.

CREATE RELATIONSHIPS WITH YOUR AUDIENCE: DAVID WANTS TO OFFER DIGITAL THINGS ONLINE IN ORDER TO GENERATE MONEY. HE WAS AWARE THAT HE FIRST NEEDED TO CULTIVATE A DEVOTED FOLLOWING. HE THEN LAUNCHED A BLOG AND STARTED POSTING HELPFUL INFORMATION THAT WAS DESIGNED TO AID OTHERS. IN ADDITION, DAVID INTERACTED WITH HIS AUDIENCE BY RESPONDING TO ALL EMAILS AND COMMENTS. HIS AUDIENCE WAS ANXIOUS TO PURCHASE HIS DIGITAL PRODUCT WHEN IT WAS FINALLY PUBLISHED, AND HE MADE A TON OF MONEY.

THE TAKEAWAY: IF YOU WANT TO EARN MONEY ONLINE, YOU MUST ESTABLISH RELATIONSHIPS WITH YOUR AUDIENCE. YOU CAN BUILD A DEVOTED FOLLOWING THAT WILL SUPPORT YOUR BUSINESS BY ADDING VALUE AND INTERACTING WITH YOUR AUDIENCE.

THERE ONCE WAS A WOMAN BY THE NAME OF SARAH WHO MADE MONEY ONLINE BY SELLING HER OWN JEWELRY. ALTHOUGH SHE WAS PROSPERING, SHE WAS AWARE THAT SHE COULDN'T RELY JUST ON ONE SOURCE OF MONEY. SARAH MADE THE DECISION TO LAUNCH A YOUTUBE CHANNEL WHERE SHE WOULD POST HOW-TO GUIDES FOR MAKING JEWELRY. SHE ALSO ESTABLISHED A PODCAST IN WHICH SHE CONDUCTED INTERVIEWS WITH OTHER JEWELRY DESIGNERS. SARAH EVEN CREATED AN ELECTRONIC BOOK ABOUT THE DEVELOPMENT OF JEWELRY. SARAH WAS ABLE TO INCREASE HER ONLINE EARNINGS BY VARYING HER SOURCES OF INCOME.

THE KEY TO EARNING MONEY ONLINE IS TO DIVERSIFY YOUR SOURCES OF INCOME. EXPAND THE RANGE OF YOUR OFFERINGS AND LOOK INTO DIFFERENT REVENUE STREAMS.

The Above used 3.5, and I will put four below so you can see the difference, but I will only show one result in the future.

ChatGPT:

CERTAINLY, LET'S MAKE THESE CONCEPTS MORE ACCESSIBLE THROUGH STORYTELLING.

1. IDENTIFY YOUR MARKET: THINK OF THIS LIKE A TREASURE HUNT. IMAGINE YOU'RE AN EXPLORER IN A NEW LAND FILLED WITH DIVERSE TRIBES, EACH WITH THEIR UNIQUE CUSTOMS AND DESIRES. YOUR MISSION IS TO IDENTIFY WHICH TRIBE YOU'RE MOST EQUIPPED TO SERVE. JUST AS AN EXPLORER WOULD STUDY AND UNDERSTAND THE TRIBES, YOU NEED TO THOROUGHLY RESEARCH AND UNDERSTAND YOUR POTENTIAL ONLINE AUDIENCE.

2. FIND YOUR NICHE: THIS IS AKIN TO BEING A CRAFTSMAN IN A MEDIEVAL TOWN. IF YOU'RE A BLACKSMITH, AND THE TOWN ALREADY HAS SEVERAL OF THEM, YOUR CHANCES OF MAKING A LOT OF MONEY ARE SLIM. HOWEVER, IF YOU SPECIALIZE IN CRAFTING BEAUTIFUL HORSESHOES, SOMETHING OTHER BLACKSMITHS AREN'T DOING, YOU'LL ATTRACT ALL THE HORSE OWNERS IN TOWN TO YOUR DOOR. LIKEWISE, IN THE ONLINE WORLD, SPECIALIZING IN A SPECIFIC AREA (YOUR NICHE) CAN HELP YOU STAND OUT FROM THE COMPETITION AND ATTRACT YOUR IDEAL CUSTOMERS.

3. BE PERSISTENT: IMAGINE YOU'RE A FARMER. YOU'VE PLOUGHED YOUR FIELD, SOWED THE SEEDS, AND NOW YOU'RE WAITING FOR THE CROPS TO GROW. YOU CAN'T RUSH IT; YOU NEED PATIENCE. SOME DAYS IT RAINS, OTHER DAYS, IT'S TOO HOT, AND PESTS ARE

ALWAYS A CONCERN. BUT YOU PERSEVERE, TEND TO YOUR FIELD, AND EVENTUALLY, YOU'LL HAVE A BOUNTIFUL HARVEST. IN THE WORLD OF ONLINE BUSINESS, YOU'LL FACE NUMEROUS CHALLENGES, BUT IF YOU'RE PERSISTENT AND WORK DILIGENTLY, THE REWARDS CAN BE SUBSTANTIAL.

4. INNOVATION AND RISK-TAKING: PICTURE YOURSELF AS AN INVENTOR. YOU'VE SEEN THAT PEOPLE STRUGGLE TO CARRY THEIR SHOPPING HOME. YOU IMAGINE A CART THAT COULD HELP. IT'S RISKY – IT MAY NOT WORK, PEOPLE MAY NOT LIKE IT, BUT YOU DECIDE TO CREATE IT ANYWAY. YOU INVENT THE SHOPPING CART, AND SUDDENLY, EVERYONE WANTS ONE. YOU'VE TAKEN A RISK, BUT THE REWARD IS IMMENSE. SIMILARLY, IN THE DIGITAL WORLD, THE KEY TO SUCCESS OFTEN LIES IN INNOVATIVE SOLUTIONS TO EVERYDAY PROBLEMS.

REMEMBER, THE INTERNET IS A VAST MARKETPLACE WITH UNBOUNDED POTENTIAL. WITH THE RIGHT APPROACH, ANYONE CAN CARVE OUT THEIR CORNER AND THRIVE. IT'S ALL ABOUT UNDERSTANDING YOUR AUDIENCE, FINDING YOUR UNIQUE OFFERING, BEING PERSISTENT, AND DARING TO INNOVATE.

Whatever skill set you may want to use; entrepreneur, freelancer, digital marketing, advertising, lead generation, video blogger, copywriting, coding, creating art, creating ads, creating blog content, writing books, SEO? — any issues or concerns you had been a thing of the past with ChatGPT.

ChatGPT can perform these tasks and more; you must use the appropriate prompt(s). This will significantly reduce the time you spend thinking about the unimportant components of the business and free up your time to focus on the customer or the areas you enjoy.

Let's say you want to dive deeper into the suggestion of making money selling products online.

PROMPT: which products should I sell online?

This prompt is very vague and will return responses to help you think and develop your ideas, which is powerful. But read further for even more powerful tricks.

ChatGPT:

IT CAN BE DIFFICULT TO CHOOSE WHICH PRODUCTS TO OFFER ONLINE, BUT THERE ARE A FEW THINGS TO TAKE INTO ACCOUNT:

SELLING GOODS THAT ARE IN LINE WITH YOUR HOBBIES AND ABILITIES CAN MAKE YOUR JOB MORE ENJOYABLE AND HELP YOU MAKE WISER DECISIONS. FOR INSTANCE, IF YOU ENJOY TAKING PICTURES, YOU MIGHT THINK ABOUT SELLING CAMERA GEAR OR PROVIDING PHOTOGRAPHY SERVICES.

DEMAND AND TRENDS: SEEK OUT GOODS THAT ARE BOTH IN GREAT DEMAND AND ON THE RISE. TO FIND POPULAR PRODUCTS AND DECIDE IF THERE IS A MARKET FOR THEM, USE GOOGLE TRENDS, AMAZON'S BEST SELLER LIST, OR SOCIAL MEDIA CHANNELS.

PROFIT MARGIN: TAKE INTO ACCOUNT THE PRODUCTS' PROFIT MARGINS WHEN MAKING YOUR DECISION. LOOK FOR THINGS THAT CAN BE OFFERED AT A HIGHER PRICE WHILE YET HAVING A LOW COST OF GOODS SOLD (COGS).

COMPETITION: CONSIDER THE LEVEL OF COMPETITION IN THE MARKET. TO FIND OUT WHAT PRODUCTS AND PRICING OTHER MERCHANTS ARE OFFERING, TRY GOOGLE SHOPPING, AMAZON, OR EBAY.

CONSIDER THE SIZE, FRAGILITY, WEIGHT, AND SHIPPING AND HANDLING NEEDS WHEN CHOOSING A PRODUCT, AS WELL AS HOW IT WILL BE SHIPPED AND HANDLED. MAKE SURE YOU CAN DELIVER YOUR GOODS TO CUSTOMERS INEXPENSIVELY AND SAFELY.

IN THE END, IT'S CRUCIAL TO DO YOUR RESEARCH AND PICK GOODS THAT ARE IN HIGH DEMAND, HAVE SIGNIFICANT PROFIT MARGINS, AND ARE ENJOYABLE TO WORK WITH. TO EFFECTIVELY MARKET AND SELL YOUR PRODUCTS, YOU MUST ALSO HAVE A SOLID MARKETING STRATEGY AND A WELL-DESIGNED ONLINE STORE.

PROMPT: Which products should I sell online to make 2,000 dollars a day, working 10 hours a week that are technology-based?

ChatGPT:

IT'S AN AMBITIOUS AMBITION TO MAKE $2,000 PER DAY WORKING ONLY 10 HOURS PER WEEK, BUT HERE ARE SEVERAL TECHNOLOGY-RELATED THINGS YOU MIGHT THINK ABOUT SELLING:

MOBILE APPLICATIONS: YOU CAN MAKE MOBILE APPLICATIONS AND SELL THEM ON APP STORES LIKE APPLE'S APP STORE AND GOOGLE PLAY IF YOU HAVE PROGRAMMING AND APP DEVELOPMENT EXPERTISE. THE APP CAN BE MADE MONEY FROM THROUGH IN-APP PURCHASES, SUBSCRIPTIONS, OR ADVERTISEMENTS.

SOFTWARE: IF YOU ARE KNOWLEDGEABLE IN A PARTICULAR FIELD, YOU CAN MAKE AND SELL SOFTWARE ONLINE. THROUGH YOUR WEBSITE OR ON RETAILERS' WEBSITES LIKE AMAZON OR EBAY, YOU CAN SELL THE SOFTWARE.

E-COMMERCE PLATFORMS: YOU CAN CONSTRUCT YOUR OWN E-COMMERCE PLATFORM AND MARKET IT TO BUSINESSES IF YOU HAVE EXPERIENCE DESIGNING AND DEVELOPING E-COMMERCE PLATFORMS. THE PLATFORM CAN BE MADE PROFITABLE BY SUBSCRIPTION FEES, TRANSACTION FEES, OR ADVERTISEMENTS.

ONLINE COURSES: IF YOU ARE A SPECIALIST IN A PARTICULAR FIELD, YOU CAN DEVELOP ONLINE COURSES THAT YOU CAN SELL TO THOSE WHO WANT TO ACQUIRE THE SAME KNOWLEDGE. IT'S SIMPLE TO

DESIGN AND SELL YOUR COURSE, THANKS TO PLATFORMS LIKE UDEMY AND COURSERA.

AFFILIATE MARKETING: THIS METHOD OF EARNING MONEY IS ALSO AVAILABLE. THIS ENTAILS MARKETING THE GOODS OF OTHER BUSINESSES ON YOUR WEBSITE OR THROUGH SOCIAL MEDIA IN EXCHANGE FOR A COMMISSION ON EACH TRANSACTION THAT RESULTS FROM YOUR REFERRAL.

REMEMBER THAT ACHIEVING THE DIFFICULT OBJECTIVE OF EARNING $2,000 PER DAY WITH ONLY 10 HOURS OF WORK PER WEEK MAY REQUIRE TIME AND EFFORT. IT'S CRUCIAL TO PICK A PRODUCT FOR WHICH YOU HAVE ABILITIES AND ENTHUSIASM, AND TO HAVE A SOLID MARKETING PLAN TO MARKET AND SELL YOUR PRODUCT EFFECTIVELY.

The days of laboriously crafting emails that took hours are long gone. If you want to email a possible client as an insurance agency, you must ask ChatGPT. Try this example below or create one that makes sense to you and your business or business ideas.

PROMPT: Write a marketing email for an insurance agency to a prospective customer

ChatGPT: (Get used to typing in the prompt on your computer) What was your result?

Suppose it was like mine; then it was a good starting point if you struggle with what to write. Here is another example of an email demonstrating how simple it is to modify the prompt and make it applicable to a different business.

I created an email for a Digital Marketing Company in less than a minute. You can send it with just some small changes.

PROMPT: Write a cold email to a potential client for a Digital Marketing Company.

ChatGPT:

SUBJECT: BOOST YOUR ONLINE PRESENCE WITH OUR DIGITAL MARKETING SERVICES

DEAR [CLIENT NAME],

I HOPE YOU ARE WELL AND READING MY EMAIL. I AM THE FOUNDER OF [YOUR DIGITAL MARKETING COMPANY NAME] AND GO BY THE NAME OF [YOUR NAME].

THROUGH SMART DIGITAL MARKETING, WE SPECIALIZE IN ASSISTING COMPANIES LIKE YOURS TO ENHANCE THEIR ONLINE PRESENCE AND INCREASE LEAD GENERATION.

I CAME ACROSS YOUR WEBSITE AND WAS [SPECIFICALLY STATE SOMETHING ABOUT THEIR PRODUCTS/SERVICES, CONTENT, OR STYLE] THAT PARTICULARLY PLEASED YOU. TO REACH A LARGER AUDIENCE, I SAW THAT YOUR WEB PRESENCE COULD BE INCREASED.

IN RESPONSE OUR TEAM OF SPECIALISTS CAN DEVELOP A SPECIFIC DIGITAL MARKETING PLAN FOR YOUR COMPANY THAT TAKES INTO ACCOUNT THE FOLLOWING:

• SEARCH ENGINE OPTIMIZATION (SEO) TO RAISE YOUR WEBSITE'S PPC (PAY-PER-CLICK) POSITION ON GOOGLE ADVERTISING TO BRING IN MORE RELEVANT VISITORS TO YOUR WEBSITE

• UTILIZING SOCIAL MEDIA TO INTERACT WITH YOUR AUDIENCE AND SPREAD BRAND RECOGNITION

• USING CONTENT MARKETING TO POSITION YOUR COMPANY AS A THOUGHT LEADER IN YOUR SECTOR

TO NURTURE LEADS AND TURN THEM INTO CUSTOMERS, USE EMAIL MARKETING

WE WOULD LOVE TO ASSIST YOUR COMPANY EXPERIENCES THE SAME
KIND OF TREMENDOUS GROWTH THAT WE HAVE HELPED COMPANIES
IN FIELDS SIMILAR TO YOURS ACHIEVE. OUR TRACK RECORD OF
SUCCESS SPEAKS FOR ITSELF.

PLEASE LET ME KNOW IF YOU'RE INTERESTED IN FINDING OUT MORE
ABOUT OUR OFFERINGS AND HOW WE CAN ASSIST YOU IN ACHIEVING
YOUR INTERNET MARKETING OBJECTIVES. I'D BE PLEASED TO SET UP
A CALL SO WE CAN TALK MORE.

BEST REGARDS,

[YOUR NAME]

This is okay, especially if you are having trouble, but we can
show you how to improve. Make it more engaging and
personable, for example.

PROMPT: Write a cold email to a potential client so they can
discover the digital marketing edge their business needs with
[Company Name]

What response did you get? Ensure you are typing this or more
specific prompts as you read into your ChatGPT.

ChatGPT:

SUBJECT: UNLEASHING YOUR BUSINESS'S POTENTIAL WITH [COMPANY
NAME]'S UNIQUE DIGITAL MARKETING STRATEGIES

DEAR [CLIENT'S NAME],

I HOPE THIS MESSAGE FINDS YOU WELL. MY NAME IS [YOUR NAME]
AND I AM [YOUR POSITION] AT [COMPANY NAME]. I CAME ACROSS
[CLIENT'S BUSINESS NAME] WHILE CONDUCTING MARKET RESEARCH
AND WAS IMPRESSED BY THE EXCEPTIONAL SERVICE YOUR COMPANY
PROVIDES.

OUR TEAM AT [COMPANY NAME] SPECIALIZES IN PROVIDING TOP-TIER DIGITAL MARKETING SOLUTIONS TO BUSINESSES AIMING TO REACH GREATER HEIGHTS IN TODAY'S DIGITAL ERA. WE OFFER A SUITE OF SERVICES, FROM SEARCH ENGINE OPTIMIZATION TO SOCIAL MEDIA MANAGEMENT, TO HELP COMPANIES EXPAND THEIR DIGITAL FOOTPRINT AND, IN TURN, DRIVE SUBSTANTIAL GROWTH.

I UNDERSTAND THAT IN TODAY'S INCREASINGLY DIGITAL MARKETPLACE, IT CAN BE CHALLENGING TO STAND OUT AMONGST THE COMPETITION. WITH OUR EXPERTISE, WE BELIEVE WE CAN ASSIST [CLIENT'S BUSINESS NAME] IN BREAKING THROUGH THIS BARRIER. WE PRIDE OURSELVES ON DEVELOPING TAILORED STRATEGIES THAT RESONATE WITH OUR CLIENTS' SPECIFIC NEEDS AND OBJECTIVES.

I BELIEVE THAT [CLIENT'S BUSINESS NAME] COULD GREATLY BENEFIT FROM OUR PERSONALIZED DIGITAL MARKETING STRATEGIES AND THAT WE COULD POTENTIALLY COLLABORATE TO UNLOCK NEW GROWTH OPPORTUNITIES FOR YOUR BUSINESS.

WOULD YOU BE AVAILABLE FOR A 15-MINUTE CALL NEXT WEEK TO DISCUSS HOW WE CAN HELP BOOST [CLIENT'S BUSINESS NAME]'S ONLINE PRESENCE? I WOULD BE DELIGHTED TO SHARE HOW WE HAVE ASSISTED SIMILAR COMPANIES IN ENHANCING THEIR DIGITAL MARKETING STRATEGIES.

THANK YOU FOR CONSIDERING OUR SERVICES. I LOOK FORWARD TO THE POSSIBILITY OF WORKING TOGETHER.

BEST REGARDS,

ChatGPT addresses the receiver personally and expresses a sincere interest in their business and well-being. As you can imagine, this applies to any business.

ChatGPT's customer care multilingual support can assist clients who speak various languages. ChatGPT could translate communications between languages and be trained in various languages, enabling efficient communication between customers and enterprises.

PROMPT: Can you respond to the following consumer query in English, French, Spanish, and Japanese with first-rate customer service? What qualities and advantages come with buying this product?

ChatGPT:

ENGLISH:

WE APPRECIATE YOUR INTEREST IN OUR OFFERING IN ENGLISH. [LIST OF FEATURES] IS JUST ONE OF OUR PRODUCT'S ATTRIBUTES. YOU CAN PROFIT FROM [LIST OF PERKS] BY PURCHASING OUR GOODS. PLEASE REMEMBER TO ASK AN ADDITIONAL QUESTIONS IF YOU HAVE ANY.

FRENCH:

MERCI DE VOUS INTÉRESSER À NOTRE PRODUIT ! LES CARACTÉRISTIQUES DE NOTRE PRODUIT INCLUENT [LIST OF FEATURES]. EN ACHETANT NOTRE PRODUIT, VOUS POUVEZ PROFITER DES AVANTAGES DE [LIST OF BENEFITS]. SI VOUS AVEZ D'AUTRES QUESTIONS, N'HÉSITEZ PAS À DEMANDER.

SPANISH:

¡GRACIAS POR SU INTERÉS EN NUESTRO PRODUCTO! LAS CARACTERÍSTICAS DE NUESTRO PRODUCTO INCLUYEN [LIST OF FEATURES]. AL COMPRAR NUESTRO PRODUCTO, PUEDE DISFRUTAR DE LOS BENEFICIOS DE [LIST OF BENEFITS]. SI TIENE MÁS PREGUNTAS, NO DUDE EN PREGUNTAR.

JAPANESE:

当社の製品にご興味いただきありがとうございます。当社の製品の特徴には、[LIST OF FEATURES] が含まれています。当社の製品を購入することで、[LIST OF BENEFITS] の利点を享受することができます。他にもご質問がある場合は、お気軽にお問い合わせください。

We no longer must do business in our city or state; we can be anywhere and make more money online. ChatGPT may be trained using client information like purchase history and chat history. Using client feedback, each customer's profile will be unique. ChatGPT can respond to a customer's message with pertinent information about their requirements and preferences.

ChatGPT can be taught to recognize and respond to common consumer grievances like poor product quality, slow shipping, or incorrect billing. When a client makes a complaint, ChatGPT can review the submission and provide a response acknowledging the customer's issues and offering potential fixes.

ChatGPT can create unique email templates for customers using the supplied client information. ChatGPT can use a template to produce an email tailored to the client's unique needs and interests when a business must contact a client.

PROMPT: Could you write a customer service email to someone having trouble contacting our service because of a heavy workload?

ChatGPT:

SUBJECT: YOUR INQUIRY TO [COMPANY NAME]: WE'RE HERE TO HELP

DEAR [CUSTOMER'S NAME],

FIRSTLY, I WOULD LIKE TO EXPRESS MY SINCERE APOLOGIES FOR ANY DIFFICULTY YOU'VE EXPERIENCED IN REACHING OUR CUSTOMER SERVICE TEAM RECENTLY. WE VALUE YOUR TIME AND YOUR BUSINESS, AND WE ARE TRULY SORRY FOR ANY INCONVENIENCE THIS MAY HAVE CAUSED.

AT [COMPANY NAME], WE ARE CURRENTLY EXPERIENCING AN UNUSUALLY HIGH VOLUME OF CUSTOMER INQUIRIES, WHICH HAS EXTENDED OUR RESPONSE TIME. PLEASE REST ASSURED, WE'RE DILIGENTLY WORKING TO ADDRESS THIS ISSUE AND IMPROVE OUR SERVICE RESPONSE TIMES.

YOUR CONCERN IS IMPORTANT TO US, AND WE WANT TO ENSURE IT IS ADDRESSED APPROPRIATELY. IF YOU COULD KINDLY PROVIDE MORE DETAIL ABOUT THE ISSUE YOU'RE FACING, I WILL PERSONALLY ENSURE THAT YOUR QUERY IS PRIORITIZED.

ALTERNATIVELY, WE CAN ALSO ARRANGE A CONVENIENT TIME FOR A MEMBER OF OUR TEAM TO CALL YOU DIRECTLY, IN CASE YOU PREFER TO DISCUSS THE MATTER OVER THE PHONE.

WE TRULY APPRECIATE YOUR UNDERSTANDING DURING THIS TIME. YOUR PATIENCE IS INVALUABLE, AND WE ARE COMMITTED TO PROVIDING YOU WITH THE LEVEL OF SERVICE YOU EXPECT AND DESERVE FROM [COMPANY NAME].

THANK YOU FOR YOUR CONTINUED SUPPORT, AND WE LOOK FORWARD TO RESOLVING YOUR QUERY AS SWIFTLY AS POSSIBLE.

BEST REGARDS,

[YOUR NAME] [YOUR POSITION] [COMPANY NAME] [YOUR CONTACT INFORMATION]

[COMPANY NAME]

If you've ever created a YouTube video or a podcast, you know how much work goes into it. What if you could produce it better and faster using ChatGPT? Starting to see how this platform can help almost every business idea of making money online? Before you even start recording - you must write a compelling introduction to hook the viewer, organize the script into a logical structure with headings and subheadings, use simple and easy-to-understand language, create a call-to-action to subscribe to your channel, rehearse, edit, optimize the script for SEO, and keep the tone, language, and message of your channel consistent.

You can also create a Script for a YouTube video or a podcast you're trying to build into your social media presence. Consider how helpful using the blog article you created to generate a video/podcast can be. You can use the existing content you generated for a blog outline and turn it into a script you can read and post on any video platform.

To fully utilize these technologies, ChatGPT is essential in creating the ideal script and instruction videos. Remember the importance of voice-overs, a crucial component of any video production. ChatGPT can help you write a perfect script, and text-to-speech software will enable you to produce a voice-over that is flawlessly delivered quickly.

Use ChatGPT to create polished scripts and instructions, as well as to generate keywords for better SEO. You may have a voiceover prepared and a video script available in seconds. The results will be better the more specific your directions are. Remember that demand for video creation is huge since people prefer watching to reading.

PROMPT: using the five informal blogs copied above, please create a step-by-step, detailed, and engaging YouTube video script.

ChatGPT:

SURE! THE FOLLOWING IS A SCRIPT FOR THE "HOW TO BUY THE PERFECT LAPTOP WITHOUT LOSING YOUR MIND" YOUTUBE VIDEO, WHICH WILL WALK

VIEWERS THROUGH EACH STAGE IN-DEPTH AND KEEP THEIR ATTENTION:

INTRO:

HEY, HOWDY, DUDES! GREETINGS FROM OUR CHANNEL ONCE MORE. WE'RE GOING TO DISCUSS PURCHASING A LAPTOP, ONE OF THE TRICKIEST CHORES IN THE COMPUTER WORLD, TODAY. THIS VIDEO IS FOR YOU IF YOU'VE EVER FOUND YOURSELF TRYING TO DECIDE WHICH LAPTOP TO PICK FROM A WALL OF COMPUTERS. YOU CAN FIND THE IDEAL LAPTOP WITHOUT LOSING YOUR MIND IF YOU USE OUR FIVE SIMPLE SUGGESTIONS. THEN LET'S GET GOING!

FIRST TIP: HOW TO GET A GREAT LAPTOP DEAL WITHOUT GIVING YOUR SOUL TO THE TECHNOLOGY GODS

BUYING A GOOD LAPTOP DOESN'T HAVE TO COST A FORTUNE. IN FACT, THERE ARE SEVERAL WAYS TO GET A GREAT DEAL WITHOUT SETTLING FOR INFERIOR GOODS.

FOR DISCOUNTS ON LAPTOPS, VISIT ONLINE RETAILERS LIKE AMAZON, BEST BUY, AND NEWEGG. ADDITIONALLY, YOU CAN SUBSCRIBE TO EMAIL NEWSLETTERS TO LEARN ABOUT UPCOMING SALES.

ON COMPUTERS THAT HAVE BEEN REPAIRED OR OPENED BUT NEVER USED, YOU MAY FREQUENTLY FIND EXCELLENT DEALS. JUST BE CAREFUL TO CHECK THE WARRANTY AND PURCHASE FROM A RELIABLE SOURCE.

NEVER HESITATE TO BARGAIN WITH THE MERCHANT OR SALESMAN. BY SIMPLY ASKING, YOU MIGHT BE ASTONISHED AT HOW MUCH MONEY YOU CAN SAVE.

TIP #2: HOW TO MAINTAIN THE VITALITY OF YOUR LAPTOP. YOU WANT TO MAKE SURE YOUR IDEAL LAPTOP LASTS AS LONG AS POSSIBLE ONCE YOU'VE FOUND IT. HERE ARE SOME POINTERS FOR MAINTAINING THE TOP CONDITION OF YOUR LAPTOP:

REGULARLY CLEAN YOUR LAPTOP WITH A MICROFIBER CLOTH, AND USE COMPRESSED AIR TO REMOVE ANY DUST OR DEBRIS FROM THE KEYBOARD AND VENTS.

NEVER LEAVE YOUR LAPTOP OUTSIDE IN THE COLD OR IN A HOT AUTOMOBILE. EXTREME TEMPERATURES HAVE THE POTENTIAL TO HARM THE BATTERY AND OTHER PARTS.

ANTIVIRUS SOFTWARE INSTALLATION BY USING A RELIABLE ANTIVIRUS TOOL, YOU CAN SHIELD YOUR LAPTOP AGAINST VIRUSES AND MALWARE. THERE ARE MANY FREE ALTERNATIVES AVAILABLE, INCLUDING AVAST AND AVG.

TIP #3: THE SEARCH FOR THE PERFECT LAPTOP: A TRIAL-AND-ERROR PROCESS

IT DOESN'T HAVE TO BE A DIFFICULT AND DRAWN-OUT PROCEDURE TO PURCHASE A LAPTOP.

DETERMINE YOUR LAPTOP'S INTENDED USE (SUCH AS GAMING, JOB, OR SCHOOL) AND SELECT ONE WITH THE SPECIFICATIONS THAT ARE APPROPRIATE FOR YOUR REQUIREMENTS.

READ EVALUATIONS DON'T MERELY FOLLOW THE SALESPERSON'S RECOMMENDATIONS. TO LEARN MORE ABOUT THE RELIABILITY AND PERFORMANCE OF THE LAPTOP, READ ONLINE USER REVIEWS.

BEFORE YOU CHOOSE, IF AT ALL FEASIBLE, CHECK OUT A FEW LAPTOPS IN PERSON. MAKE SURE THE KEYBOARD, SCREEN, AND OVERALL FEEL OF THE LAPTOP ARE COMFORTABLE FOR YOU.

TIP #4: THE PC VS. MAC GREAT LAPTOP DEBATE. THE CHOICE BETWEEN A PC AND A MAC IS ONE OF THE MOST IMPORTANT ONES YOU'LL HAVE TO MAKE WHEN PURCHASING A LAPTOP. HERE ARE A FEW BENEFITS AND DRAWBACKS OF EACH:

PCS TYPICALLY COST LESS AND HAS A WIDER SELECTION OF BRANDS AND MODELS.

THE DURABILITY, DEPENDABILITY, AND USER-FRIENDLY INTERFACE OF MACS ARE WELL RENOWNED. WHILE MACS ARE SUPERIOR FOR ARTISTIC TASKS LIKE GRAPHIC DESIGN AND VIDEO EDITING, PCS ARE BETTER FOR GAMING AND CUSTOMIZING.

TIP #5: A CRASH COURSE IN LAPTOP BUYING FOR THE TECH-CHALLENGED

DON'T WORRY IF YOU'RE UNFAMILIAR WITH THE WORLD OF COMPUTERS.

If you need more information or the script generated isn't long enough, just type, "Please rewrite it to be 200 words longer with more detail on [topic]."

I still need to put the ChatGPT response here; you could change the prompt and use it to create a video script on any topic and length.

Social media marketing is a must for any entrepreneur or business owner. Whether you run your social media marketing or outsource the work to an agency is quite competitive. Keeping up with all the updates on social media sites can be a real burden.

Keeping up with the newest developments and trends in social media marketing is crucial. You want to stay caught up in the field because it always evolves. Developing interesting material that appeals to your target audience might be challenging. Social media marketing ROI measurement can take much work. The effect of social media activities on a company's bottom line is difficult to quantify. It might be challenging to manage client expectations.

As your company expands, managing a team can become a real challenge. Social media experts might need help to work with. Creativity and strategy must be balanced. You must create interesting, original material that advances a client's commercial objectives. Delivering results for clients while staying within budget can take much work. You're constantly looking for new material to offer to your clientele. You can boost conversions and drive sales for your clients and your business by utilizing ChatGPT to create expert-caliber content.

CHAPTER 5

Use ChatGPT to Become a Top Earner Online

I hope you are like I was and excited to experience the power of ChatGPT, the ultimate tool to help you generate a steady stream of passive income effortlessly. Discover the ultimate strategies to boost your income and ascend to the pinnacle of the online content creation and freelancer pay scale.

Distinguishing yourself in a specific niche is a proven strategy to differentiate yourself from competitors and attract top-tier clients willing to pay a premium. From finance and investing to health and fitness, the possibilities are endless. Position yourself as an expert in a specific area of interest and watch as your client base grows. Focus on a particular topic to establish authority and attract a wider audience.

Unlock the potential of social networking sites such as Facebook, LinkedIn, and Twitter to generate leads and attract customers effortlessly. Maximize your potential for attracting new business by frequently sharing your ChatGPT-generated content and engaging with your fans. Develop a strong online presence that will set you apart from the competition.

Showcasing your skills and expertise through high-quality samples is a powerful tactic for attracting valuable clients. Elevate your chances of securing new clients by showcasing your worth through top-notch samples that rival or surpass your competitors.

Stay updated with the latest trends and best practices in online content creation by networking with fellow ChatGPT users. Furthermore, establishing connections with potential customers interested in your services can be beneficial.

Discover how content creators and freelancers can leverage ChatGPT to create content and generate income in multiple ways. Unlock a world of possibilities with this technology, enabling you to create chatbots, virtual assistants, and customer support services. Maximize your business's efficiency by utilizing it to craft compelling content, from breaking news to engaging social media updates. Save valuable time and resources with this powerful tool.

With ChatGPT, you can effortlessly create exceptional and one-of-a-kind content for your blog, articles, product descriptions, and social media posts. With ChatGPT, writers can effortlessly tap into a wealth of inspiration and ideas to elevate their work. Alternatively, they can delegate some of their research and writing tasks to ChatGPT, freeing up valuable time.

By implementing these proven tactics, elevate your ChatGPT earnings and position yourself as a leading earner in online content creation and freelancing. Deliver exceptional content and unparalleled customer support, and financial rewards will follow.

Discover new project concepts and brainstorm ideas effortlessly with ChatGPT. Harness its power to create cutting-edge solutions for your client's challenges. With ChatGPT, you can effortlessly schedule appointments, send invoices, and manage client conversations all in one place.

Unlock the potential of ChatGPT by crafting bespoke models tailored to specific markets or sectors. With ChatGPT, you can conduct thorough and efficient research on topics that cater to your clients' needs. Save time and elevate your work with this solution.

Follow the most recent ChatGPT developments and try out new features and methods. By doing this, you'll be able to maintain your competitive edge and give your customers the greatest support.

Using ChatGPT as a freelancer can help you advance your profession and increase your income.

Here are a few pieces of advice:

- Use ChatGPT for idea generation and brainstorming. ChatGPT can help you develop original, cutting-edge solutions for your clients, making you stand out as a talented freelancer. Your ability to write and communicate will increase due to your interaction with ChatGPT, which will also be helpful to your freelance business.

- Ensure that you're using these tools morally and legally correct, as this was also tempting to me. This involves observing data privacy laws and abstaining from all forms of discrimination.

- Understanding and utilizing ChatGPT's (and other AI's) limitations is crucial. It doesn't take the role of human wisdom and discretion. Think about how your client views AI and how it might influence their company. Be open about using these technologies and address your client's concerns, as some individuals may be reluctant to adopt AI-powered products or services.

- ChatGPT can be used for research and fact-checking to save time and increase productivity. ChatGPT can help you obtain and verify the information for your clients. As ChatGPT develops and improves, keeping up with new features and capabilities will help you stay competitive in the freelance market.

- For improving the pace and effectiveness of your online freelance work, ChatGPT can be a great tool. Using its language creation features, you may easily create high-quality material, such as articles, blog entries, and social media posts. Because of the time you'll save, you can work with more clients and earn more money.

- Learning to appropriately input prompts and modify the output to suit your needs is crucial to utilize ChatGPT's capabilities fully. Additionally, you can use it for research and data analysis, enabling you to gather information and derive insights quickly for your work.

It's critical to remember that even though ChatGPT can make your work go more quickly, maintaining high standards is still crucial. Always check the output for accuracy, relevance, and compliance with your or your client's needs first. You can become skilled at utilizing ChatGPT to generate high-quality work in less time with practice and experience.

Fast-thinking freelancers are better at engaging clients and meeting their needs. ChatGPT's reminders, scheduling, and organizing capabilities improve project management. These freelancer tools boost productivity and customer happiness. Stay organized and do chores quickly. Increase efficiency and workflow to raise profits and freelance status.

Provide additional training to all AI tools to boost everyone's knowledge of business-specific jargon. Add chatbots or virtual assistants to ChatGPT for a complete solution. Organizations may automate their processes and streamline operations with our cutting-edge automation technologies.

ChatGPT lets you train unique models on specific datasets for precise and relevant responses. This tool lets you easily customize AI replies. Customize the language, tone, and topic to your liking. Create customer service and interaction models that match customer preferences. Models can help bloggers and writers create original content. Custom models can automate data analysis and translation.

ChatGPT's custom model-building capability gives users a strong tool to improve the AI's capabilities and tailor its replies to their requirements. Users can fine-tune the model to produce solutions most pertinent to their needs by training it on data sets. Unique models can be developed for various use cases, like customer service, commerce, or creative writing. Users can ensure that the responses generated by ChatGPT are highly tailored and in line with their business objectives by training the model on specific data sets. Businesses may benefit by improving consumer engagement, boosting sales, and increasing productivity.

ChatGPT can be integrated with other software and solutions to improve functionality and capabilities. ChatGPT, for instance, can relate to chatbots, virtual assistants, and messaging programs to give users more precise and pertinent responses. Automate content production and curation; it can also relate to content management systems. To offer insights and forecasts based on sizable data sets, ChatGPT can also relate to data analytics tools. Users can increase their productivity and efficiency while boosting the accuracy and relevance of the AI's responses by integrating ChatGPT into other applications and tools.

With ChatGPT, users can build chatbots and virtual assistants offering individualized help and support. Developing intelligent agents that can comprehend and reply to user inquiries in natural language is feasible by training ChatGPT on domains and tasks. This can enhance user experience while assisting businesses and organizations in automating customer service and support. A few platforms and devices can access chatbots and virtual assistants developed using ChatGPT by integrating them with messaging services, websites, and mobile applications.

Before using ChatGPT, decide what your goals are and how you plan to use the tool. This will enable you to select and modify the ideal model for your requirements. To get the most out of ChatGPT, the model needs to be practiced using pertinent data. Text, pictures, and other information can be a part of this. The model will be more accurate the more data you submit. ChatGPT is a strong instrument, but the best results necessitate trial and error. Try several prompts and adjust the model to get the desired results.

With ChatGPT, you can become a top-earning freelancer. To be clear, using ChatGPT does not excuse you from doing any work; rather, it enhances and amplifies your current skill sets to produce significantly more high-quality material in the same amount of time.

Some content creation markets are about to transform; many services now have lower entry barriers. We learned how to compose blog posts by creating titles, outlines, and the post itself.

ChatGPT allows you to publish well-researched, educational, and interesting blog posts, articles, or books in a fraction of the time it would take you to write them from scratch. ChatGPT can assist you in creating informative and shareable material for your website or a blog for a customer.

As we've seen, ChatGPT allows you to write five hundred words in only minutes, whereas most people would need hours or even days to complete the task. The first chapter demonstrates how simple it is to create a book outline.

A well-written, informative eBook can be created with ChatGPT in a fraction of the time it would take you to compose one from scratch. Additionally, you'll be able to delight your customers and keep them coming back for more because ChatGPT can assist you in creating more interesting and well-written content.

With ChatGPT, while it will take some time, you will accomplish these tasks in a matter of hours which most others take weeks to do successfully. Even though you can't just ask ChatGPT to write the entire book for you, you can use the same process we used to outline this book, then write the chapter summaries, and then write the actual chapters; with a little editing, it only takes a few hours, which isn't too bad.

PROMPT: create a 10-chapter outline for a blog post with the title [insert your book title here] on [topic].

PROMPT: write a chapter 1 more detailed outline

PROMPT: write the above chapter in the manner of [a favorite author] in a captivating tone. And make it 2,000 words.

Do the above three Prompts using your blog or eBook that you want to write or read. One issue to keep in mind while writing content if a book is that ChatGPT can only produce up to ~3000 words in one response. However, this problem can be easily fixed by suggesting to keep going or giving me more information.

Let's discuss keyword research now.

PROMPT: what keywords should I include in the content on a blog post about SEO maximization

ChatGPT:

HERE ARE SOME KEYWORDS YOU COULD INCLUDE IN A BLOG POST ABOUT SEO MAXIMIZATION:

SEARCH ENGINE OPTIMIZATION (SEO)

KEYWORDS

ON-PAGE OPTIMIZATION

OFF-PAGE OPTIMIZATION

META TAGS

LINK BUILDING

CONTENT OPTIMIZATION

SITE ARCHITECTURE

USER EXPERIENCE (UX)

MOBILE OPTIMIZATION

LOCAL SEO

ANALYTICS

RANK TRACKING

ALGORITHM UPDATES

BACKLINKS

SOCIAL MEDIA OPTIMIZATION (SMO)

CONVERSION OPTIMIZATION

ORGANIC TRAFFIC

PAID SEARCH

It's essential to seamlessly integrate these keywords into your text rather than forcefully inserting them just for the sake of it. Deliver valuable, top-notch content that caters to the requirements of your target audience while adhering to the search engine algorithms' standards.

Use effective SEO (Search Engine Optimization) tactics and strategies to enhance your website's visibility and ranking. Optimize your blog's SEO by utilizing ChatGPT to verify specific keywords and phrases for your text. Discover the power of keywords - the specific words and phrases that individuals use to seek out content akin to yours on the vast expanse of the internet. Elevate your website's search engine ranking by seamlessly incorporating relevant keywords into your blog posts.

Even ask ChatGPT about long-tail keywords, which are precise and in-depth phrases people use to search for topics, which are some of the crucial keywords to add to blog material for SEO optimization. LSI (Latent Semantic Indexing) keywords, which are associated with the primary keyword and add extra context and relevance to the content, are additional significant keywords. To increase the visibility of the blog article, keywords must also be used in the header tags, meta description, and title.

The quantity and caliber of the material, the use of internal and external links, and the inclusion of multimedia components like photographs and videos are additional characteristics that affect SEO optimization. In addition, the content has to be interesting, relevant, and informative for the intended audience. You can raise your website's position, boost traffic, and attract more potential consumers by incorporating these crucial keywords and adhering to SEO best practices. ChatGPT can help do it better and faster.

Rest assured; the outcome will require only minor editing and proofreading. With ChatGPT, you can elevate your ad campaigns to new heights! Create expertly crafted written content that will captivate your audience and drive conversions. Let ChatGPT be your go-to solution for crafting persuasive ad copy, regardless of platform, from landing pages to banner ads to social media promotions. Imagine a situation where a valued client requires an email marketing campaign to promote the release of their latest product.

With ChatGPT, you can gain the competitive edge you need to distinguish yourself and command top rates for your services, regardless of whether you're a seasoned veteran or a newcomer to the online business arena. Experience lightning-fast and precise document creation, top-notch content writing, and unparalleled coding for your one-of-a-kind projects with ChatGPT.

CHAPTER 6

Use ChatGPT to Develop Valuable Recurring Streams of Passive Income

ChatGPT empowers you to craft diverse content that can generate recurring passive income streams. With ChatGPT, you have the power to craft profitable content with e-books, courses, and training materials. With ChatGPT, you can effortlessly craft engaging blog entries, captivating social media updates, and various other types of content that can be monetized through affiliate marketing, sponsored content, and other lucrative avenues. Elevate your status and cultivate a loyal customer base with ChatGPT's ability to help you with content creation services. Establish yourself as a trusted industry expert and attract potential buyers or clients eager to invest in your exceptional products and services. With the right approach, this technique can help you generate long-term passive income streams that evolve and expand over time.

Discover the benefits of ChatGPT for enterprising freelancers and visionary entrepreneurs. Unlock your full potential as a freelancer or business owner with ChatGPT. ChatGPT is here to help you streamline your processes and free up your time to focus on the critical work that requires your unique skills and expertise. Let ChatGPT handle the automation of certain tasks so you can maximize your productivity and achieve your business goals. Revolutionize your idea-generation process with ChatGPT!

Maximize your productivity and take your business to the next level with ChatGPT. Unlock your full freelancer or business owner potential with ChatGPT's powerful features and functionalities. Gain a competitive edge in your field and achieve success like never before.

Discover and refine your digital product concept with the help of ChatGPT's investigative and developmental capabilities. Let ChatGPT help you with brainstorming and product idea development by generating relevant data and ideas. With ChatGPT, you can elevate your product to new heights with exceptional content creation, stunning graphic design, and impeccable product formatting services. Whatever your product or service may be, ChatGPT can help you as it did with me.

Maximize the potential of your digital product with ChatGPT's expert market research and tailored marketing plan. Let us help you reach your target audience and achieve your business goals. Discover your ideal audience, create engaging social media posts and ads, and cultivate effective email marketing strategies with ChatGPT.

Leverage the power of ChatGPT to analyze valuable customer feedback and product suggestions and take your offering to the next level. Discover the optimal price point for your product through strategic experimentation with pricing strategies and leveraging the powerful insights provided by ChatGPT to analyze customer behavior and feedback.

Boost your chances of success and establish a steady stream of passive income with ChatGPT. ChatGPT can assist in generating leads by reviewing consumer inquiries and recommending tailored solutions or goods. You can save time and effort while boosting your income potential by implementing ChatGPT into your digital marketing plan. ChatGPT can be a valuable tool in your quest for financial independence with the appropriate attitude and direction.

Strategies for marketing and selling your items to create passive revenue with ChatGPT

Utilize social media platforms for a successful marketing and sales strategy for digital products made with ChatGPT. Connect with more people and communicate with them using social media to reach a larger audience. Create social media profiles for your company and use them to promote your brand, present your products, and give your fans helpful content.

Offering free trials or samples of your digital products is an additional tactic. This enhances the likelihood that a potential customer will purchase by enabling them to try before they buy. Create a teaser for your product or produce and provide a free chapter of your eBook using ChatGPT.

Using email marketing can also help you increase revenue and cultivate a following of devoted customers. Use ChatGPT to develop tailored email campaigns that address client groups, such as those who have already expressed interest in your products. To maximize the possibility of conversions, ensure your emails are engaging, educational, and pertinent to your client's needs.

You may reach a larger audience and spark interest in your items by working with influencers. Use ChatGPT to find potential influencers, get in touch with them, and forge a productive alliance. This may be a potent strategy for boosting sales and brand recognition.

Tips for developing valuable and marketable products with ChatGPT

Your target market's needs must be considered when creating content and ideas with ChatGPT. Concentrate on producing informative, original content that addresses issues or offers answers. Use conversational and understandable language. Before making your content available to the public, test it on a limited group to ensure it works. The target market's needs must be considered when creating goods with ChatGPT.

Concentrate on producing informative, original content that addresses issues or offers answers. To develop valuable and marketable products with ChatGPT, consider your target audience and their needs, use clear and concise language, provide relevant and useful information, and ensure your product is visually appealing. Using ChatGPT to create material that can be sold, such as podcasts, courses, and eBooks, is one approach to achieve this. You can rapidly and effectively generate high-quality material with ChatGPT's brainstorming tools. Have you tried to use ChatGPT for your specific needs yet? Stop reading for a little while and practice your prompts.

Once developed, you can utilize ChatGPT to market and promote your content. You may find new clients and produce efficient marketing messages with ChatGPT. ChatGPT can automate marketing initiatives like sending emails or posting on social media.

Making and selling chatbots or virtual assistants is another option for using ChatGPT to generate passive income. Virtual assistants and chatbots are gaining popularity across various industries, including customer service, healthcare, and banking. You may use ChatGPT to build chatbots and virtual assistants that are very intelligent and attentive to user needs.

ChatGPT can create, and market customized models to other companies or people. Custom models can be applied to various tasks, including sentiment analysis, predictive analytics, and language translation. You can generate passive income while assisting others in sophisticated problem-solving by designing and selling custom models.

Do you like stocks and investments? Create an Indicator for Trading Bots. Indicators, which are used to assess market data and produce indications for automated trading systems, are one of the significant characteristics of trading bots. It may be a fundamental indicator, a technical indicator, or a hybrid of the two. Technical indicators produce trading indications through mathematical calculations based on market information like price and volume. On the other hand, fundamental indicators use data on the company and the macroeconomic environment to produce indications.

PROMPT: develop a prescriptive indicator that sends out a buy signal when volume rises by 10% over 60 minutes.

ChatGPT: What did you put as your PROMPT? What was the response? Do you need more information? Just ask ChatGPT.

A crucial step in data analysis is creating dashboards or visualizations, which may be used to communicate findings and predictions to others. You may assist businesses and organizations in understanding their data and making better decisions by developing a service that produces these data visualizations or dashboards.

The use of ChatGPT can be beneficial to software development in a variety of ways. It might start by offering technical guidance and insight, assessing code, and resolving code issues to assist with software development. By utilizing these characteristics, the software development process may be expedited, and productivity boosted.

Programs that require natural language processing can be developed using the ChatGPT API. Additionally, ChatGPT may offer beneficial code samples in any programming language using a text prompt that lists the application's demands. You could develop this for yourself or make money creating software for others.

A broad category includes digital assets. It has a variety of works, such as a collection of icons, texture images, and a sophisticated design system. It counts as a digital asset if you create something that consumers desire, anything that makes it easier or faster for designers to work. For instance, you can have it generate picture sets of icons, Web flow plugins for Sigma, scripts for Sketch, templates, mockups, 3D objects, and templates for presentations using flowcharts.

ChatGPT unlocks passive revenue! Our user-friendly software lets anyone duplicate good chances hundreds or thousands of times. Take your chance to earn more with less work. ChatGPT now! Save time making AI art to sell on stock photo websites. Millions of people are flooding these industries, and many are being banned. Target better-paying, less-crowded positions.

It's essential in a saturated market. Participate despite competition. Instead, carefully distinguish your work. Compete fiercely.

ChatGPT unlocks passive income streams for uncomplicated moneymaking. ChatGPT offers unlimited content monetization options. Your works can be sold or used to drive people to your website or social media accounts, where you can make significant money through affiliate marketing or advertising.

ChatGPT can let you profit from your interest! eBooks and online courses on topics you love can earn passive money. ChatGPT makes eBook and course writing easy. It's quick and effective.

ChatGPT's affiliate program unlocks passive money. ChatGPT lets you write engaging product reviews and promotional content with affiliate links. Increase revenue and website traffic today! Customers who buy through your links get commissions.

ChatGPT makes it easy to create engaging content for your website or social media accounts that generates cash through advertising. ChatGPT's high-quality content draws visitors to your website or social media profiles. Use Google AdSense to monetize website traffic. Profit now!

ChatGPT lets you build several passive income streams. ChatGPT unleashes your talents and passions! Our platform lets you easily make money from your expertise. Our top-notch article production services allow you to ditch traditional labor and earn without effort.

Concentrate on things that, even with ChatGPT, will take some time to do well, things that can't be generated perfectly in one prompt. The market will be balanced; it will stand out if you take your time producing high-quality material. Concentrate on eBooks, Blog Posts, YouTube Videos, Online Courses, and Software Applications. eBooks can be a big source of passive income even though they require much upfront work. With Amazon Publishing, you can also make your book available in print without worrying about contracts with traditional publishing houses.

Fortunately, ChatGPT can assist you with many of these; let's begin with identifying a niche. If you are still figuring out where to write, you might have a brainstorming session to develop ideas.

PROMPT: What are some good unique niches to write an eBook in ChatGPT?

ChatGPT:

HERE ARE SOME UNIQUE NICHES THAT YOU COULD CONSIDER WHEN WRITING AN EBOOK:

SUSTAINABLE LIVING: AS THE WORLD BECOMES MORE ENVIRONMENTALLY CONSCIOUS, PEOPLE ARE LOOKING FOR WAYS TO REDUCE THEIR IMPACT ON THE PLANET. AN EBOOK ON SUSTAINABLE

LIVING COULD COVER TOPICS SUCH AS ECO-FRIENDLY HOME IMPROVEMENTS, ZERO-WASTE LIVING, OR REDUCING PLASTIC USAGE.

ChatGPT came up with six other ideas and then said these are only a few instances of distinctive niches that you might consider when producing an eBook. The secret is to choose a subject you and your audience will be interested in.

Then your process should be to pick one; let's use the first one and drill down further.

Prompt: give me some topics I can write about in sustainable living.

ChatGPT:

HERE ARE SOME TOPICS YOU CAN WRITE ABOUT IN SUSTAINABLE LIVING:

SUSTAINABLE HOME IMPROVEMENT: ADVICE ON HOW TO MAKE CHANGES TO YOUR HOME THAT ARE MORE ENVIRONMENTALLY FRIENDLY, SUCH AS INSTALLING ENERGY-EFFICIENT FIXTURES OR RAINWATER COLLECTION SYSTEMS.

ZERO WASTE LIVING REFERS TO PRACTICES LIKE COMPOSTING, UTILIZING REUSABLE CONTAINERS, AND SHOPPING IN BULK THAT HELP YOU CREATE LESS WASTE EVERY DAY. YOU MIGHT OFFER ADVICE ON MINIMIZING PAPER, CLOTHES, AND FOOD WASTE.

USING NATIVE PLANTS, COMPOSTING, AND STAYING AWAY FROM PESTICIDES AND COMMERCIAL FERTILIZERS ARE JUST A FEW SUSTAINABLE GARDENING TIPS. ANOTHER THING YOU MAY DO IS TEACH PEOPLE HOW TO GROW THEIR OWN FOOD, WHETHER IT BE IN A BACKYARD GARDEN OR A CONTAINER.

GREEN TRANSPORTATION: METHODS FOR LOWERING YOUR CARBON FOOTPRINT THAT DON'T INCLUDE DRIVING, SUCH TAKING THE BUS, BIKING, OR WALKING. YOU MIGHT ALSO GIVE ADVICE ON CHOOSING A MORE FUEL-EFFICIENT CAR AND ELECTRIC VEHICLE.

SUSTAINABLE FASHION: ADVICE FOR BUILDING A MORE ENVIRONMENTALLY FRIENDLY WARDROBE INCLUDES BUYING USED CLOTHING, SELECTING NATURAL FIBERS, AND SPENDING MONEY ON HIGH-QUALITY ITEMS THAT WILL ENDURE FOR A LONG TIME. ADDITIONALLY, YOU MIGHT TALK ABOUT ETHICAL FASHION LABELS AND THE EFFECTS OF FAST FASHION ON THE ENVIRONMENT.

SUSTAINABLE TRAVEL: STRATEGIES FOR MINIMIZING YOUR IMPACT ON THE ENVIRONMENT WHILE TRAVELING, SUCH AS PICKING ECO-FRIENDLY LODGING, ASSISTING NEIGHBORHOOD BUSINESSES, AND USING THE BUS. YOU MIGHT ALSO OFFER DETAILS ON VOLUNTEERISM AND SUSTAINABLE TRAVEL.

SUSTAINABLE FOOD REFERS TO METHODS FOR MINIMIZING YOUR ENVIRONMENTAL EFFECT THROUGH YOUR DIETARY CHOICES, SUCH AS FOLLOWING A PLANT-BASED DIET, PURCHASING ORGANIC AND LOCALLY GROWN FOOD, AND CUTTING BACK ON FOOD WASTE. YOU MIGHT ALSO TALK ABOUT THE EFFECTS OF INDUSTRIAL AGRICULTURE ON THE ENVIRONMENT AND SUSTAINABLE FARMING METHODS.

THESE ARE JUST A FEW IDEAS FOR TOPICS YOU CAN WRITE ABOUT IN SUSTAINABLE LIVING. THE KEY IS TO CHOOSE A TOPIC THAT YOU ARE PASSIONATE ABOUT AND THAT WILL RESONATE WITH YOUR AUDIENCE.

Now you can select a topic that makes sense for you want to write on. Let's use the sustainable home improvement example provided above. And now, let's focus on how we can start working on a book outline with the help of our new AI friend.

PROMPT: create an outline for a book on Sustainable home improvement

ChatGPT: I have not included the response, but what did you get? And you can be as specific as you want or need depending on what you want to write.

This outline would offer a fundamental framework for a book on environmentally friendly home improvement. Of course, the author's objectives and intended audience can and should influence the precise subjects covered and the depth of material offered.

Please remember that this is only an example outline and that your research and target audience may need you to add or remove a few things. Additionally, you can expand each section's subtopics based on your needs. We can now generate chapter outlines using the book outline.

You can do a prompt to create an outline for Chapter 1 in the book *Sustainable Home Improvement*. Ask ChatGPT to write a 200-word introduction to the book using the above chapter outline, etc.

You can even go deeper and ask to suggest a few appropriate book titles and subtitles for this book. And even ask it to create a descriptive and engaging sales page for the book. It almost makes me want to buy this book myself or, better yet, create and sell it. See how easy this can be to make money online with ChatGPT?

Let's talk more about a book marketing e-mail. This is one of the big benefits of ChatGPT. Without adding more information, you can ask it to create a marketing email for the book it just helped you write. And now we can get its help to create a Twitter announcement.

Prompt: Create a Twitter announcement for the release of the book

ChatGPT:

YES, HERE IS AN EXAMPLE TWEET ANNOUNCING THE PUBLICATION OF THE BOOK:

"FANTASTIC NEWS! SUSTAINABLE HOME IMPROVEMENT, OUR NEW BOOK, IS NOW AVAILABLE! DISCOVER HOW TO BUILD AN ECO-FRIENDLY HOME USING REAL-WORLD ADVICE, TACTICS, AND CASE STUDIES. #SUSTAINABLE #HOMEIMPROVEMENT" "GET YOUR COPY TODAY AND JOIN THE MILLIONS OF INDIVIDUALS IMPROVING THE ENVIRONMENT."

ChatGPT can also give you marketing emails like the one above and so much more. We can even work with ChatGPT to help guide you with pricing based on your target market and marketplace to optimize sales. I hope you can start to feel how powerful this tool can be for you, making even more money online.

YouTube videos are suitable for passive income because your catalog of videos is valuable as time goes on, as any new audience that finds you would be interested in your old content and can keep generating ad revenue for years afterward. And this is in stark contrast to social media posts which can have a shelf life of a few hours, depending on the platform. Let's say you're unsure of what videos to create; maybe you have a niche or don't. It would work best if you have a topic you know or have experience in, but let's ask ChatGPT for help developing a niche or topic to explore.

Prompt: Give me some ideas about low-competition keywords for a YouTube video on Sustainable Home Improvement.

What did you get as a response from ChatGPT? Was it enough for you? If not, ask again or ask for more details. Practice asking more detailed questions or adding to your original Prompts.

To be sure that these keywords are low competition and have the potential to rank well on YouTube, conduct some additional research and assess their search traffic and competitiveness using other online keyword tools.

How about you ask it to generate an engaging and humorous script? So, it will generate a little short for 10 minutes and need some editing but a good starting point, especially if you're facing writer's block. Usually, you'd have to do the video recording. Still, if you don't like being on camera or would rather have a video created for you that you are can then voiceover, you're in luck, as there is a tool called **Pictory** that even uses AI to generate a full video with images and text based on a script or even a blog that you feed into it. You can then read over it without ever showing your face, or should you choose, use one of their inbuilt AI voice characters to voice your video. However, YouTube videos with AI are rarely monetized, so if that is your goal, you are better off creating the video and then doing the voiceover to make more money online with AI and YouTube.

We've gone through ideas from brainstorming keywords and titles to generating the full post and YouTube Videos, so now we'll focus on creating blog posts more specifically tailored for affiliate marketing. Like YouTube videos, good blogs have a long shelf life and can be an income source that lasts many years.

ChatGPT is, without a doubt, a game-changer for affiliate marketers. It transforms the writing process and how we interact with people. It can also be utilized to conduct in-depth market research and develop creative new ideas for engaging your target audience.

You can also utilize the ChatGPT-based Bing assistant, which the same AI language model drives. Bing has the added advantage of allowing live internet searches, but its response options are more constrained. Using both tools in tandem is the best strategy.

ChatGPT has remarkably impacted various professions, particularly those involved in content creation, such as affiliate marketers. The ultimate question is, are you maximizing its benefits? Experience will be a learning curve, as with any innovative technology., so start practicing now and continue it daily. Starting a blog has always been challenging with cutting-edge technologies like ChatGPT. While top-notch content is essential, blogging is ultimately a game of numbers. Unlock the power of ChatGPT to effortlessly generate a plethora of top-notch articles over and over again that will last and help you make money online in perpetuity. ChatGPT empowers individuals to produce articles at a rate that previously demanded a full team.

CHAPTER 7

Limitations of ChatGPT for Making Money Online

Discover the power of ChatGPT and realize it can be the ultimate solution for creating amazing content that can help you earn big bucks online. Like any tool, it does come with certain limitations. Discover the essential limitations before depending excessively on ChatGPT for your online earnings.

While it has many strengths, one of the critical limitations of this product is its inability to provide the same level of creativity and personalization as a human. Using ChatGPT, you must understand that figurative language, such as sarcasm or irony, can sometimes lead to miscommunications or imprudent reactions and content.

While ChatGPT is an incredibly advanced tool, it is designed to supplement human creativity and innovation. While it can generate text based on prompts, it cannot generate innovative concepts or employ non-traditional approaches. In today's competitive online market, it's crucial to differentiate yourself from the rest. To make an impact, consider infusing your unique flair into ChatGPT's impressive output.

ChatGPT is famous for its fast and accurate text production. It has been used for writing essays and curating social media content but has limitations. ChatGPT is a great communication tool. However, it cannot understand language. It can write grammatically and semantically correct terminology but may not convey the intended tone or context. Thus, it may only sometimes convey language, dialect, or cultural nuances. Unfortunately, this can lead to misinterpretations and communication failures in the corporate world, especially with international audiences.

Experience personalized conversations like never before with ChatGPT! While it has its strengths, there may be better options for client-facing responsibilities that require a personal touch and empathetic approach. ChatGPT's effectiveness in generating ideas or content may be limited in languages or cultures not included in its training data, as it has been specifically trained using language and cultural data.

ChatGPT may only suit some companies or industries as a burgeoning technology. Custom AI models tailored to their specific needs may be necessary for businesses with unique challenges or obstacles. Many companies must invest heavily in database accuracy and completeness to gain important insights from data analysis. ChatGPT combines cutting-edge technology and human skills for the best conversation experience.

Despite its limitations, ChatGPT is useful for creating corporate content and improving teamwork. Grammar, punctuation, and syntax elements improve writing. ChatGPT helps you create a convincing pitch by merging powerful facts and information. A good pitch requires understanding the audience, finding the main message, and telling a compelling story. ChatGPT can help with technical writing but not pitch writing. Use ChatGPT's cutting-edge technology and human inventiveness to maximize corporate content production and program building. ChatGPT is the best AI tool for brainstorming and creativity! ChatGPT's cutting-edge technology lets you improve your message like never before.

While ChatGPT boasts impressive capabilities, it does have its limitations. Discover the potential limitations of ChatGPT, as with any AI technology, that may affect its precision and effectiveness. Discover the potential of ChatGPT to boost your revenue! However, combining it with other tools and tactics is crucial while considering its limitations to maximize its benefits.

Although our model can provide responses that mimic human-like conversation and has access to vast amounts of information, it needs to catch up in the realm of common sense. Additionally, ChatGPT needs to gain background knowledge of being human. ChatGPT's responses to certain questions or situations may occasionally be nonsensical or inaccurate. While ChatGPT can offer valuable ideas and resources, it may not match human minds' boundless creativity and originality. This factor may limit the potential for creating unique and attractive products and content.

While it can generate grammatically correct and pleasing content, it may only sometimes be accurate or appropriate in its context. Ensure the accuracy and relevance of the data provided to your audience.

The quality of ChatGPT's prompts may impact its performance. Keep low-quality prompts from hindering your ChatGPT results. Crafting exceptional prompts tailored to your unique requirements is of utmost importance. The last chapter of this book and the free book on the first page will give you so many prompts to try, but practice and come up with the best prompts.

ChatGPT is encountering challenges in producing extensive and well-structured written material. Although the model can generate coherent and grammatically sound sentences, producing extensive content that adheres to a specific structure, format, or storyline may encounter difficulties. ChatGPT is the perfect solution for creating concise content such as summaries, bullet points, or brief explanations. Requesting multiple tasks simultaneously may hinder its ability to prioritize, reducing efficiency and precision.

Discover the transparency of ChatGPT! Occasionally, the AI may produce responses that are inadvertently biased or discriminatory. While ChatGPT boasts an impressive database, it's important to note that it cannot match the vast knowledge and experience of human beings. While ChatGPT is incredibly knowledgeable, it may have some of the answers regarding highly specialized or niche topics. Additionally, it may need to be updated on the latest developments or changes in certain fields.

ChatGPT's capacity to detect typos, grammatical errors, and misspellings is somewhat restricted. While the model can generate technically correct responses, it may only sometimes be accurate in context or relevance. Processing complex or specialized information can be daunting, especially when accuracy and precision are paramount. This limitation poses a significant challenge in such scenarios. Ensure the accuracy of

ChatGPT's generated information by taking necessary verification measures.

Unlock the full potential of ChatGPT for your unique needs by fine-tuning the model to achieve optimal results. Refining your model through fine-tuning is a meticulous process that requires training it on a specific dataset to enhance its performance for a particular task or objective. However, this process can be quite demanding regarding time and resources.

Experience the power of ChatGPT, a cutting-edge AI language model that boasts unparalleled sophistication and complexity. However, the model demands significant computational resources to ensure optimal performance, which may translate to higher operational costs and the need for specialized hardware and software systems. Experience faster processing times, improved accuracy, and optimal performance by running ChatGPT on high-end hardware or systems with advanced computational power. Running ChatGPT on low-end hardware or systems with limited computational power may reduce performance and other related issues. Before utilizing ChatGPT, organizations must evaluate their computational resources and capabilities thoroughly.

While ChatGPT is an effective solution for many, it may only suit some people's needs. Certain markets and sectors reap greater advantages from it than others. It is of utmost importance to acknowledge the limitations of ChatGPT and consider alternative tools and approaches that can bolster its effectiveness in your industry.

While ChatGPT is an exceptional tool for creating top-notch content and generating passive income streams, it's important to note that it's not a cure-all solution. Unlock the full potential of your internet business by acknowledging its limitations and utilizing it judiciously.

While ChatGPT strives to deliver precise and reliable results, errors and imprecisions remain possible, particularly in intricate undertakings such as legal or medical composition. Exercise caution when relying solely on ChatGPT's content.

Unlock the full potential of ChatGPT to take your business to new heights! While it's an incredibly valuable tool for firms of all sizes, maximizing its benefits can come at a cost. The cost may seem exorbitant for those seeking to monetize ChatGPT-generated content, particularly for small organizations or individuals.

Unlock the full potential of your business or personal brand by leveraging the power of cutting-edge technology. You can create top-tier content that drives revenue and generates buzz with the right combination of tools and resources, including skilled human editors and translators. It's crucial to break down extensive inquiries into bite-sized portions and sequentially enter them for optimal outcomes. Despite its drawbacks, ChatGPT remains an invaluable tool for individuals seeking to generate income online.

Discover effective ways to guarantee the ethical and responsible use of ChatGPT. Discover the full potential of ChatGPT. Unleash the power of ChatGPT to connect with people from all over the world. Join the conversation and exchange ideas with like-minded individuals. Experience the convenience of our user-friendly interface and enjoy seamless communication. For optimal and safe utilization, it is imperative to exercise ethical and responsible conduct while leveraging the power of

ChatGPT. Discover the ethical principles of using ChatGPT that will help you distinguish between acceptable and unacceptable uses. While ChatGPT can offer inspiration and resources, it may not match human beings' boundless creativity and originality. This factor may limit the potential for creating unique and attractive products.

Experience the precision you deserve with ChatGPT's enhanced accuracy. While it can create grammatically correct and engaging content, it may only sometimes align with the appropriate context or factual accuracy. Ensure the accuracy and relevance of the data provided to your audience.

Although ChatGPT touts outstanding speed and quality in generating content, the text may only sometimes correspond with the intended message or the tone the organization wants to convey. Developing content for certain markets or industries that use sophisticated terminologies and jargon can be a more challenging writing endeavor.

Companies require cutting-edge technology and valuable human expertise to grow. ChatGPT is useful but cannot replace human imagination, instinct, and emotional intelligence in creating a truly appealing message. Businesses may create a memorable experience by combining cutting-edge technology and human inventiveness as these streamlines procedures and maximize human potential.

When it comes to the topic of making money online, ChatGPT has its drawbacks, even though it is undeniably a great tool for improving both productivity and the quality of the content that is produced. Utilizing ChatGPT in conjunction with human ingenuity and grasping the limits imposed by it might help you protect yourself from potential threats.

CHAPTER 8

Best Practices for ChatGPT Success

Use ChatGPT to increase production, earnings, and efficiency. However, use it wisely. Review the last chapter and observe its limits to maximize your ChatGPT experience. Use AI-generated content to enhance productivity and grow your online business. ChatGPT is the breakthrough platform that lets you easily write great blog posts, comments, and content for articles or books on any topic.

Like any technology, ChatGPT's issues and recommended techniques must be carefully considered to enhance your experience. With the content in this book and my free prompts, you will be able to maximize ChatGPT.

Set up your account to optimize workflow and integrate ChatGPT with other tools and services. Choose prompts and parameters to simplify your experience. ChatGPT can help you improve your writing, increase your internet footprint, and sell your content. Optimize your experience and maximize our platform. No matter your field, succeed easily, join ChatGPT's successful users worldwide, and boost your online profile.

Training and refining your ChatGPT model choices for each project will maximize its potential. The prompts that I share are designed to give you the background you need to succeed. Learn to write your prompts with perfect grammar and sentence structure.

Find the right prompt format and delivery method for you. Experiment to discover your perfect fit. Add ChatGPT to your toolkit to boost productivity. Monitor and evaluate ChatGPT results to maximize your potential. Keep up with ChatGPT updates to improve performance.

Know your goals before using ChatGPT. Optimize tool proficiency and results. Consistency is power. Like any tool, use ChatGPT to its greatest capacity. Use it often to learn its full potential.

ChatGPT lets you design customizable models. This powerful tool lets you create custom models for your business.

Check ChatGPT usage results often to see what works. Use this knowledge to improve your strategy and results. ChatGPT boosts productivity and workflow. Integrating ChatGPT with other automation technologies boosts efficiency. Discover how ChatGPT may raise productivity and income with your current toolbox.

Another book I wrote, *How to Sell Your Business Without a Business Broker,* was made even better by asking for good direct prompts. I didn't want it to be it for me, but I was able to verify and validate that I was headed in the best direction using ChatGPT. The first use case was to ensure my outline was valid.

PROMPT: can you improve my outline (Input the outline into the prompt)

CERTAINLY, HERE'S AN IMPROVED OUTLINE WITH A FEW MODIFICATIONS AND REORGANIZATION FOR CLARITY:

CHAPTER 1: INTRODUCTION

CHAPTER 2: BUSINESS VALUATION

CHAPTER 3: PREPARING FOR SALE

CHAPTER 4: EXECUTIVE SUMMARY AND CONFIDENTIAL INFORMATION MEMORANDUM (CIM)

CHAPTER 5: BUYER SEARCH AND PRESCREENING

CHAPTER 6: INITIAL CONTACT AND DISCUSSION

CHAPTER 7: PRICING AND DEAL STRUCTURING

CHAPTER 8: LETTER OF INTENT - OFFER TO PURCHASE

CHAPTER 9: BUYER DUE DILIGENCE

CHAPTER 10: PURCHASE AGREEMENT AND CLOSING

CHAPTER 11: SELLER'S KIT AND NEXT STEPS

I HOPE THIS REVISED OUTLINE HELPS YOU IN ORGANIZING AND WRITING YOUR BOOK.

This helpful insight ensured that I had included everything I needed to complete the book and that I could add or change some of my chapters.

Discover ChatGPT's untapped capacity to boost efficiency, profits, and workflow. Use it carefully. Rereading the next few chapters a few times and noting their limitations will improve your ChatGPT experience.

Consider ChatGPT's issues and recommended methods to maximize your experience as with any technology. This book and my free prompts will help you maximize ChatGPT's capabilities. Master the skill of writing intriguing and polished prompts for the best content that profoundly resonates with readers.

Integrate ChatGPT with your many products and services to simplify your process. Choose prompts and parameters that enhance your experience. ChatGPT unleashes your writing. Uncover ChatGPT's best practices! Learn how to maximize your experience and maximize our platform. Find effortless success as a blogger, marketer, business owner, or content provider. Join the global ChatGPT community of successful users and transform your online profile!

To ensure precision, write instructions with perfect grammar and sentence structure. Review and improve your material. Unleash your creativity with the proper prompt format and delivery method for your style. Explore alternatives to find your perfect mate. ChatGPT can help you work faster and wiser. Monitor and evaluate your ChatGPT scores to maximize your potential. Keep up with

Clear goals are necessary to utilize ChatGPT fully. As with any vital resource, maximize ChatGPT's potential. ChatGPT lets you customize models to your specifications. Assess ChatGPT results often to determine what works and what doesn't. Use this knowledge to improve your approach and effects as you progress. ChatGPT enhances workflow and productivity.

Integrate ChatGPT with automation technologies to boost productivity. ChatGPT unlocks your potential!

Know the latest advances that are included with ChatGPT. This cutting-edge technology is continually evolving with new features and functions. Stay ahead of the game by remaining current with this tool's capabilities. Regular practice will help you become more proficient as you utilize ChatGPT more frequently. Utilize the many features and capabilities it offers by practicing often.

By experimenting with them, see how different settings and parameters affect ChatGPT's output, but reread the first few chapters on these settings. You will better understand how to use ChatGPT efficiently for various activities.

If you experience ChatGPT errors or inaccurate output, try to determine the issue's root and take a lesson from it. This will assist you in avoiding making the same errors again.

Let's examine a technique for swiftly producing content for several social networking platforms. Assume your customer wants to introduce a new computer backpack, and you want to pitch them an advertising campaign right away. They want to know how the campaign would break down and how much it would cost. So let's design a marketing campaign with the "Act as" prompt we discussed earlier.

PROMPT: Please assume the role of a digital marketing agency. Please design a comprehensive marketing plan to support the goods or services of your choice. Select a target market, create key themes and slogans, choose the media outlets for advertising, and decide on any further actions required to meet the objectives. Give examples of the advertising costs for each social media platform and your best guess for the Cost per Click (CPM) and Cost per Thousand Impressions (CPC) costs. My first request is, "I need help creating an advertising campaign for a new type of computer backpack targeting young adults aged 22-32."

ChatGPT:

HERE IS A THOROUGH MARKETING STRATEGY FOR A NEW STYLE OF COMPUTER BAG AIMED AT YOUNG ADULTS BETWEEN THE AGES OF 22 AND 32:

YOUNG INDIVIDUALS BETWEEN THE AGES OF 22 AND 32 WHO ARE COMPUTER SAVVY AND FREQUENTLY TRAVEL WITH LAPTOPS AND OTHER ELECTRONIC DEVICES MAKE UP OUR TARGET DEMOGRAPHIC. THEY ARE DIGITAL NOMADS, YOUNG PROFESSIONALS, AND COLLEGE STUDENTS WHO PLACE A HIGH IMPORTANCE ON FASHION, CONVENIENCE, AND USABILITY.

THE FOLLOWING MESSAGES WILL BE THE FOCUS OF OUR MAIN THEMES AND CATCHPHRASES:

• THE IDEAL BAG FOR THE DIGITAL ERA

• KEEP IN TOUCH WHEN TRAVELING WITH OUR BACKPACK

• SAFEGUARD YOUR TECHNOLOGY IN STYLE.

• CLEVER DESIGN FOR CONTEMPORARY LIVING

• COMMERCIAL CHANNELS

THE FOLLOWING ADVERTISING CHANNELS WILL BE USED BY THE US TO REACH OUR TARGET AUDIENCE, SOCIAL MEDIA PROMOTION. WE'LL ADVERTISE OUR COMPUTER BACKPACK ON SOCIAL MEDIA SITES LIKE

FACEBOOK, INSTAGRAM, AND TWITTER. TO HIGHLIGHT THE FEATURES AND ADVANTAGES OF THE BACKPACK, WE'LL MIX VISUAL AND VIDEO ADVERTISEMENTS.

THE FOLLOWING ARE THE EXPECTED ADVERTISING EXPENDITURES FOR EACH PLATFORM, $0.50 TO $2.00 CPC AND $5 TO $10 CPM ON FACEBOOK. INSTAGRAM: CPMS OF $5 TO $6, CPCS OF $0.70 TO $1.00. TWITTER: $0.50–$2.00 CPC, $9–11:00 CPM. $5,000 WILL BE SET ASIDE FOR SOCIAL MEDIA ADVERTISING.

INFLUENCER MARKETING TO PROMOTE OUR COMPUTER BAG, WE WILL COLLABORATE WITH RELEVANT INFLUENCERS IN THE TECH AND FASHION DOMAINS. THEY WILL RECEIVE COMPLIMENTARY BACKPACKS, AND WE WILL ASK THEM TO POST MATERIAL ON THEIR SOCIAL MEDIA ACCOUNTS THAT HIGHLIGHTS THE BACKPACK.

INFLUENCER MARKETING IS ANTICIPATED TO COST $500 PER INFLUENCER.

WE'LL PRODUCE INTERESTING BLOG POSTS AND FILMS TO HIGHLIGHT THE CAPABILITIES AND ADVANTAGES OF OUR PC BACKPACK. THESE WILL BE POSTED ON OUR WEBSITE, SHARED ON SOCIAL MEDIA, AND PROMOTED VIA EMAIL MARKETING.

THE MONTHLY COST OF CONTENT MARKETING IS PROJECTED TO BE $1,000.

THE FOLLOWING ADDITIONAL STEPS WILL BE TAKEN BY US IN ORDER TO ACHIEVE OUR MARKETING GOALS. SHOWCASE OUR BACKPACK AT TRADE EVENTS AND CONFERENCES TO ATTRACT CUSTOMERS.

TO INCREASE SALES, GIVE NEW CLIENTS EXCLUSIVE DEALS AND OFFERS.

WORK TOGETHER WITH RETAILERS AND FIRMS TO OFFER OUR BACKPACKS IN THEIR SHOPS.

CONCLUSION

BY USING A COMBINATION OF SOCIAL MEDIA ADVERTISING, INFLUENCER MARKETING, AND CONTENT MARKETING, WE WILL SUCCESSFULLY PROMOTE OUR NEW TYPE OF COMPUTER BACKPACK TO OUR TARGET MARKET OF YOUNG ADULTS AGED 22-32. OUR ESTIMATED TOTAL ADVERTISING BUDGET IS $10,000.

This is a decent starting point. It gives you a great place to start, the key messages, and an overview of the platforms and channels to use, approximate costs, and activities. You can change the prompt to request deadlines, prices for additional channels, or even a budget allocation based on the best Return on Investment.

Suppose you establish a reusable super sponge with a smiley face that gets soft in warm water. Ask ChatGPT to create an Instagram post for this service.

PROMPT: As a digital marketing agency, create an engaging Facebook post for a reusable super sponge in the shape of a smiley face that gets soft in warm water.

ChatGPT:

LOOKING FOR A FUN AND ECO-FRIENDLY WAY TO CLEAN UP SPILLS AND MESSES AROUND YOUR HOME? CHECK OUT OUR REUSABLE SUPER SPONGE IN THE SHAPE OF A SMILEY FACE! 😊 🧽

THIS INNOVATIVE SPONGE GETS SOFT AND PLIABLE WHEN YOU SOAK IT IN WARM WATER, MAKING IT PERFECT FOR TACKLING ALL SORTS OF MESSES. AND BECAUSE IT'S REUSABLE, IT'S A GREAT WAY TO REDUCE WASTE AND DO YOUR PART FOR THE ENVIRONMENT.

WHETHER YOU'RE CLEANING UP AFTER A BIG FAMILY MEAL, WIPING DOWN YOUR COUNTERS, OR TACKLING SPILLS ON YOUR FLOORS, THIS SMILEY FACE SPONGE IS SURE TO PUT A SMILE ON YOUR FACE. SO WHY WAIT? ORDER YOURS TODAY AND SEE THE DIFFERENCE FOR YOURSELF! ☀

With ChatGPT 4, it can even add some pictures or emojis. What did you get for your project? In addition to the response to the post, I got some information from ChatGPT on when to post and how to use this, and more to better engage on Facebook. If you need more information or details, then ask ChatGPT.

PROMPT: What is the best time to run this as a Facebook post?

What was your response? Was it helpful? Do you need even more? Just ask. Mine said to run them between 10 am and 3 pm, which I would try to see if it works best or if this might need manual intervention.

The post can feature a clean and attractive set of product images or videos, a specific call to action, a sense of urgency, and a time-limited incentive. Typically, a business like this would want to be present on all social media sites and post on Twitter; you would normally have to start from scratch because the platform is unique, and the character limit is challenging to work within. But these days, you can ask ChatGPT to handle it.

PROMPT: as a Marketing Agency, repurpose this into an engaging Tweet

ChatGPT:

SURE, THERE'S AN ENGAGING TWEET FOR THE REUSABLE SUPER SPONGE IN THE SHAPE OF A SMILEY FACE:

😊 🧹 SAY GOODBYE TO BORING CLEANING WITH OUR REUSABLE SUPER SPONGE! IT'S SHAPED LIKE A SMILEY FACE AND GETS SOFT IN WARM WATER. 🐱 💙 #REUSABLESUPERSPONGE #SMILEYFACE #SUSTAINABLECLEANING #CLEANINGHACKS

Emojis and a lighthearted tone help this tweet grab the audience's attention and emphasize the salient aspects of the product. Additionally, it has pertinent hashtags to aid in boosting visibility and interaction.

Twitter's posts are shorter than Instagram's posts. The additional emojis are exciting and help the audience interested in green living feel connected. You may keep doing this by converting the original article into a post for Facebook, LinkedIn, or another platform like Pinterest or a script for a TikTok video. This can save time and guarantee that branding and tone are used consistently across all platforms with little work. Imagine you have an online shop where you offer handcrafted goods. You may generate product descriptions for Pinterest or your website using ChatGPT, raising attention and boosting sales.

Additionally, ChatGPT can be used to create email marketing campaigns that advertise your products and provide subscribers with exclusive discounts or promotions. Additionally, making exciting and shareable content for websites like Pinterest, Twitter, and Instagram is much simpler, allowing you to connect with more people and develop a strong following. If you capitalize on popular hashtags and themes, your work can go viral and gain many new viewers and exposure.

Prompt: Create a Pinterest product listing for an affordable hat

ChatGPT:

SURE, HERE'S AN EXAMPLE PINTEREST PRODUCT LISTING FOR AN AFFORDABLE HAT:

TITLE: "STYLISH AND AFFORDABLE COTTON BUCKET HAT"

INTRODUCING OUR FASHIONABLE AND REASONABLY PRICED COTTON BUCKET HAT! THIS HAT, WHICH IS MADE OF SOFT, BREATHABLE COTTON FABRIC, IS IDEAL FOR ANY OUTDOOR ACTIVITY. THIS HAT WILL KEEP YOU COOL AND SHIELD YOU FROM THE SUN WHETHER YOU'RE GOING ON A HIKE, SPENDING THE DAY AT THE BEACH, OR SIMPLY RUNNING ERRANDS AROUND TOWN.

THIS HAT, WHICH HAS A TRADITIONAL BUCKET HAT STYLE, IS BOTH PRACTICAL AND STYLISH. THE UNISEX SIZING ASSURES A COMFORTABLE FIT FOR EVERYONE, AND IT COMES IN A RANGE OF COLORS TO MATCH ANY OUTFIT. IT'S A TERRIFIC ADDITION TO YOUR SUMMER WARDROBE AND WON'T BREAK THE BANK, THANKS TO THE REASONABLE PRICE.

FEATURES SMOOTH, BREATHABLE COTTON FABRIC CONSTRUCTION.

TRADITIONAL BUCKET HAT STYLE HAS MANY DIFFERENT COLORS FOR A COMFORTABLE FIT; CHOOSE UNISEX SIZING WITH A REASONABLE PRICING RANGE

THIS HAT WILL BE SENT VIA REGULAR SHIPPING BETWEEN 1-3 BUSINESS DAYS. AT THE CHECKOUT, THERE ARE OTHER OPTIONS FOR EXPEDITED SHIPPING.

TO MAINTAIN YOUR HAT'S FINEST APPEARANCE, WE SUGGEST SPOT WASHING WITH A DAMP CLOTH AS REQUIRED. DON'T DRY OR WASH IN A MACHINE.

THANK YOU FOR CONSIDERING OUR AFFORDABLE COTTON BUCKET HAT! WE ARE CONFIDENT THAT IT WILL BECOME YOUR GO-TO ACCESSORY FOR ALL YOUR SUMMER ADVENTURES.

Please start seeing the potential for using ChatGPT in your life and with all your social media campaigns. It still amazes me what ChatGPT can develop despite having very little information.

Let's say you have a personal brand focused on selling managed services and want to increase your LinkedIn following by posting helpful information.

Prompt: In an engaging tone, please write a blog post on the importance of using managed services to protect your computer investment.

ChatGPT:

SURE, HERE'S AN ENGAGING BLOG POST ON THE IMPORTANCE OF USING MANAGED SERVICES TO PROTECT YOUR COMPUTER INVESTMENT:

"ARE YOU PROTECTING YOUR COMPUTER INVESTMENT?

WITH THE INCREASING RELIANCE ON TECHNOLOGY IN TODAY'S BUSINESS WORLD, IT'S MORE IMPORTANT THAN EVER TO ENSURE THAT YOUR COMPUTER SYSTEMS ARE SECURE AND FUNCTIONING AT THEIR BEST. THAT'S WHERE MANAGED SERVICES COME IN!

BY PARTNERING WITH A MANAGED SERVICES PROVIDER, YOU CAN ENJOY PEACE OF MIND KNOWING THAT YOUR COMPUTER INVESTMENT IS PROTECTED AND WELL-MAINTAINED. FROM PROACTIVE MONITORING TO REGULAR MAINTENANCE AND SUPPORT, MANAGED SERVICES CAN HELP PREVENT ISSUES BEFORE THEY BECOME MAJOR PROBLEMS AND KEEP YOUR SYSTEMS RUNNING SMOOTHLY.

SO DON'T WAIT UNTIL DISASTER STRIKES TO START THINKING ABOUT YOUR COMPUTER SECURITY AND MAINTENANCE. TAKE ACTION NOW AND INVEST IN

MANAGED SERVICES TO PROTECT YOUR BUSINESS'S MOST VALUABLE ASSET. 💻 🔒

#MANAGEDSERVICES #COMPUTERSECURITY #PROACTIVEMONITORING #BUSINESSTECHNOLOGY #INVESTMENTPROTECTION"

BY USING A CONVERSATIONAL TONE AND HIGHLIGHTING THE BENEFITS OF MANAGED SERVICES, THIS LINKEDIN POST EFFECTIVELY COMMUNICATES THE IMPORTANCE OF PROTECTING YOUR COMPUTER INVESTMENT. IT ALSO INCLUDES RELEVANT HASHTAGS TO HELP INCREASE VISIBILITY AND ENGAGEMENT.

As you can see, it tried to draw the reader in with the "Are you protecting your computer investment?" And pay attention to how it ended with hashtags appropriate for social platforms you could use this on.

Here we're going to create a workout plan for a 40-year-old male. This will show you why ChatGPT is so much more helpful than if you'd just googled "workout plans" because now, considering everything you entered here, including the workout plan, you can ask it to generate a tailored plan for a specific age and sex.

Prompt: As a personal trainer, give me a three-month workout plan for a 40-year-old male.

ChatGPT:

What did you get as a response? It can also give you helpful tips that maybe you didn't ask directly. It will provide tips like "As you advance over the three months, be sure to increase the weight and intensity of your workouts steadily. It's crucial to pay attention to your body's signals and take breaks as needed. To ensure perfect form and technique, consider speaking with a licensed personal trainer."

Additionally, remember that accomplishing fitness goals necessitates proper nutrition and diet. Encourage your client to maintain a balanced diet to support their exercise goals. As you can see, it specifies that diet and nutrition will complement the workout plan.

ChatGPT can be very generic or drill down and be as specific as you need or want it to be. Let's step back and assume you have no business yet or even a business idea.

PROMPT: Draft a business idea for a 50-year-old retired carpenter.

ChatGPT:

HERE'S A BUSINESS IDEA FOR A 50-YEAR-OLD RETIRED CARPENTER:

BUSINESS OF CUSTOM WOODWORKING

THE RETIRED CARPENTER CAN USE HIS CARPENTRY KNOWLEDGE AND TALENTS TO LAUNCH A CUSTOM WOODWORKING BUSINESS. THE COMPANY CAN MAKE CABINETS, FURNITURE, AND OTHER WOODEN THINGS TO ORDER FOR BOTH RESIDENTIAL AND COMMERCIAL USE.

IN ORDER TO DEMONSTRATE HIS ABILITIES AND CONSTRUCT A PORTFOLIO OF HIS WORK, THE RETIRED CARPENTER CAN START BY DESIGNING AND PRODUCING A FEW PIECES OF FURNITURE. HE CAN ALSO THINK ABOUT SETTING UP A WEBSITE OR A SOCIAL MEDIA ACCOUNT TO PROMOTE HIS SERVICES AND CONNECT WITH POTENTIAL CLIENTS.

THE RETIRING CARPENTER MIGHT NEED TO MAKE EQUIPMENT AND TOOL PURCHASES TO START THE FIRM. HE MIGHT ALSO THINK ABOUT LEASING A LITTLE WORKSHOP TO WORK ON AND SAVE HIS CREATIONS.

THE RETIRED CARPENTER CAN DEMONSTRATE HIS WORK AND BUILD RELATIONSHIPS WITH POSSIBLE CUSTOMERS BY PARTICIPATING IN REGIONAL TRADE SHOWS, FARMER'S MARKETS, OR CRAFT FAIRS TO MARKET THE BUSINESS. HE CAN USE SOCIAL MEDIA TO ADVERTISE HIS COMPANY AND REACH MORE PEOPLE.

OVERALL, FOR A RETIRED CARPENTER WHO IS PASSIONATE ABOUT WORKING

WITH WOOD AND MAKING UNIQUE ITEMS, LAUNCHING A CUSTOM WOODWORKING BUSINESS CAN BE A REWARDING AND SUCCESSFUL ENDEAVOR.

You can alter the question/prompt to elicit a different response, make it funnier or more enjoyable, add a personality trait you believe will elicit a response, or even use different authorial styles.

PROMPT: Write a cold approach email in Mark Cuban's style

It's important to note that Mark Cuban's communication style, particularly in cold emails, may not align with the professional tone you want, so pick a respected expert in your field. The email's intended audience will also affect its content, fashion, and style. But continue to type in examples and prompts for your business as we go along so all this makes more sense for you, your company, and your projects.

ChatGPT:

SURE, HERE'S AN EXAMPLE OF A COLD APPROACH EMAIL IN MARK CUBAN'S STYLE:

SUBJECT: WHY YOUR BUSINESS NEEDS TO PARTNER WITH [COMPANY NAME]

DEAR [CLIENT NAME],

I HOPE THIS EMAIL FINDS YOU WELL. MY NAME IS [YOUR NAME], AND I'M THE CEO OF [COMPANY NAME], A DISRUPTIVE DIGITAL MARKETING AGENCY THAT'S SHAKING UP THE INDUSTRY WITH OUR INNOVATIVE STRATEGIES AND FEARLESS APPROACH.

I CAME ACROSS YOUR BUSINESS AND WAS IMPRESSED WITH YOUR PRODUCTS/SERVICES AND YOUR PASSION FOR INNOVATION. I KNOW FIRSTHAND THAT IT TAKES GUTS AND DETERMINATION TO SUCCEED IN BUSINESS, AND THAT'S WHY I'M REACHING OUT TO YOU TODAY.

AT [COMPANY NAME], WE SHARE YOUR VALUES AND UNDERSTAND WHAT IT TAKES TO SUCCEED IN TODAY'S EVER-EVOLVING MARKETPLACE. OUR TEAM OF EXPERTS HAS A PROVEN TRACK RECORD OF HELPING BUSINESSES LIKE YOURS GAIN A COMPETITIVE EDGE AND ACHIEVE EXPLOSIVE GROWTH THROUGH OUR CUTTING-EDGE DIGITAL MARKETING SOLUTIONS.

WE OFFER A RANGE OF SERVICES, INCLUDING SEARCH ENGINE OPTIMIZATION (SEO), PAY-PER-CLICK (PPC) ADVERTISING, SOCIAL MEDIA MARKETING, CONTENT MARKETING, AND EMAIL MARKETING. WE USE THE LATEST TOOLS AND STRATEGIES TO HELP BUSINESSES LIKE YOURS DOMINATE THEIR NICHE AND REACH NEW HEIGHTS OF SUCCESS.

I'M A FIRM BELIEVER IN THE POWER OF COLLABORATION, AND I KNOW

You can also use this to speed up your customer service department by creating template emails. Use this as a live tool to respond to emails as they come in or generate any templates that your customer service can utilize for a particular inquiry type.

I'll offer an example below of a customer who requested a refund but violated your store's policies. For example, imagine you get inquiries from buyers who want a refund but must follow your guidelines.

PROMPT: Write a polite but firm email to a customer who requests to cancel his subscription but is informed that this is against business policy.

ChatGPT:

SURE, HERE'S AN EXAMPLE OF A POLITE BUT FIRM EMAIL TO A CUSTOMER WHO REQUESTS A REFUND BUT IS INFORMED THAT THIS IS AGAINST BUSINESS POLICY:

SUBJECT: REGARDING YOUR REQUEST

DEAR [CUSTOMER NAME],

I VALUE YOUR INTEREST IN OUR SERVICES AND YOUR EMAIL. I REGRET TO INFORM YOU THAT YOU WISH TO CANCEL YOUR MEMBERSHIP, BUT I MUST POINT OUT THAT, IN ACCORDANCE WITH BUSINESS POLICY, CANCELLATIONS MUST BE MADE AFTER THE SUBSCRIPTION PERIOD HAS ENDED.

THE GOAL OF OUR POLICY IS TO GUARANTEE THAT ALL OF OUR CLIENTS RECEIVE THE BEST SERVICE AND SUPPORT POSSIBLE FOR THE DURATION OF THEIR SUBSCRIPTIONS. WE SINCERELY HOPE YOU HAVE FOUND OUR SERVICES TO BE BENEFICIAL, AND WE WOULD BE HONORED TO CONTINUE SERVING YOU.

IF THERE IS ANYTHING WE CAN DO TO HELP YOU MAKE THE MOST OF OUR SERVICES, DO LET US KNOW. WE ARE AVAILABLE AT ALL TIMES TO ASSIST YOU AND RESPOND TO YOUR INQUIRIES.

WE APPRECIATE YOUR USING OUR SERVICES AND YOUR UNDERSTANDING.

BEST WISHES

[YOUR NAME]

[BUSINESS NAME]

This is a great, useful example that you can implement today. Did you? Can you see how this will help you in the future? This can be used by customer service in many languages for any country where you sell your service or products.

With ChatGPT, step up your freelancing game! With the aid of this cutting-edge AI tool, professionals may develop client-wowing material while earning extra money. Businesses now reward employees who use this technology to produce well-researched, polished work.

You can use ChatGPT to advertise some of the following freelance services:

• Use ChatGPT to create blog or website content.

• With CHATGPT, translate into any language.

• ChatGPT's email writing service

• ChatGPT lets you create headlines and calls to action.

• Create a YouTube video script using ChatGPT

• Write social media posts or marketing content.

• Create a short story with the help of the ChatGPT hashtag

Maximizing your blog's potential requires optimizing it for search engines. ChatGPT can assist you in enhancing your blog post's search engine optimization (SEO) to make it more discoverable. The material in this book and the free prompts will guide you on how to format your content for maximum visibility, recommend strategic keywords to enhance your blog post, and provide valuable tips to elevate your entire online profile. Expand your research and product acquisitions with just a few clicks. Try it now and discover the keywords to take your business to the next level. Don't even know where to begin, ask ChatGPT.

PROMPT: related keywords to making money online as a blogger in {TOPIC}

What response did you get for your personalized prompt? Give the AI clear and specific instructions if you want to use ChatGPT for blogging and produce original and excellent material. While writing, clearly convey the piece's intended direction and include any pertinent background information.

We all know that Google and other search engines love blog posts on your websites. Let's say you want to write an exciting blog post for your audience, but doing so requires much work and time. Select a subject that is interesting and pertinent to your target audience, do extensive research using reliable sources, and arrange the information you've gathered logically using headings, subheadings, bullet points, and numbered lists. However, much of that work can now be completed with a single click.

PROMPT: Give me five blog post suggestions for high search volume and low competition keywords for buying a new laptop

ChatGPT:

YES, HERE ARE FIVE BLOG ARTICLE IDEAS FOR TERMS CONNECTED TO PURCHASING A NEW LAPTOP THAT HAS A HIGH SEARCH VOLUME AND LITTLE COMPETITION:

"10 BEST LAPTOPS FOR COLLEGE STUDENTS ON A BUDGET" - THIS POST CAN TARGET THE HIGH SEARCH VOLUME AND LOW COMPETITION KEYWORDS "BEST LAPTOPS FOR COLLEGE STUDENTS" AND "BUDGET LAPTOPS."

"THE ULTIMATE GUIDE TO CHOOSING THE RIGHT LAPTOP FOR YOUR BUSINESS NEEDS" – THIS POST CAN TARGET THE HIGH SEARCH VOLUME AND MODERATELY COMPETITIVE KEYWORDS "BUSINESS LAPTOPS" AND "BEST LAPTOPS FOR BUSINESS".

"TOP 5 LAPTOPS FOR GRAPHIC DESIGNERS AND VIDEO EDITORS" - THIS POST CAN TARGET THE HIGH SEARCH VOLUME AND LOW COMPETITION KEYWORDS "LAPTOPS FOR GRAPHIC DESIGN" AND "VIDEO EDITING LAPTOPS."

"GAMING LAPTOPS UNDER $1000: A COMPREHENSIVE BUYING GUIDE" - THIS POST CAN TARGET THE HIGH SEARCH VOLUME AND COMPETITIVE KEYWORDS "GAMING LAPTOPS UNDER $1000" AND "BEST BUDGET GAMING LAPTOPS. "

"MAC VS. PC: WHICH IS THE BEST OPTION FOR YOU?" - THIS ARTICLE CAN TARGET THE HIGH SEARCH TRAFFIC AND COMPETITIVE KEYWORDS "MAC VS PC" AND "LAPTOPS FOR MAC USERS."

TO INCREASE YOUR CONTENT'S SEARCH ENGINE VISIBILITY, DON'T FORGET TO CONDUCT IN-DEPTH KEYWORD RESEARCH TO IDENTIFY THE MOST PERTINENT AND HIGH-PERFORMING KEYWORDS.

Prompt: create an outline for me (Reminder that you do not have to remind the AI what you were talking about).

ChatGPT,

SURE, HERE'S AN OUTLINE FOR A BLOG POST TITLED "TOP 5 LAPTOPS FOR GRAPHIC DESIGNERS AND VIDEO EDITORS":

I. INTRODUCTION

    A. BRIEF OVERVIEW OF THE IMPORTANCE OF HAVING THE RIGHT LAPTOP FOR GRAPHIC DESIGN AND VIDEO EDITING

    B. EXPLANATION OF THE PURPOSE OF THE BLOG POST: TO PROVIDE RECOMMENDATIONS FOR THE TOP 5 LAPTOPS FOR GRAPHIC DESIGNERS AND VIDEO EDITORS

    C. BRIEF OVERVIEW OF THE CRITERIA USED TO SELECT THE LAPTOPS FOR THE LIST

II. CRITERIA FOR SELECTION

    A. PROCESSOR

    B. RAM

    C. GRAPHICS CARD

    D. DISPLAY

    E. BATTERY LIFE

    F. PRICE

III. TOP 5 LAPTOPS FOR GRAPHIC DESIGNERS AND VIDEO EDITORS

    A. LAPTOP 1: [NAME OF LAPTOP]

    1. OVERVIEW OF THE LAPTOP'S SPECS AND FEATURES

    2. PROS AND CONS OF THE LAPTOP

    3. PRICE RANGE

B. LAPTOP 2: [NAME OF LAPTOP]

1. OVERVIEW OF LAPTOP'S SPECS AND FEATURES

2. PROS AND CONS OF THE LAPTOP

3. PRICE RANGE

C. LAPTOP 3: [NAME OF LAPTOP]

1. OVERVIEW OF THE LAPTOP'S SPECS AND FEATURES

2. PROS AND CONS OF THE LAPTOP (OUR HONEST OPINION)

3. PRICE RANGE (IS IT WORTH SELLING YOUR FIRSTBORN FOR?)

D. LAPTOP 4: [NAME OF LAPTOP]

E. LAPTOP 5: [NAME OF LAPTOP]

IV. CONCLUSION

A. RECAP OF THE TOP 5 LAPTOPS FOR GRAPHIC DESIGNERS AND VIDEO EDITORS

B. FINAL THOUGHTS AND RECOMMENDATIONS (WHAT WE PERSONALLY USE AND

LOVE)

C. ENCOURAGEMENT TO SHARE YOUR OWN EXPERIENCES AND OPINIONS IN THE

COMMENTS

This is factually correct and is a good start, but it may not match your style and tone, so play or practice with it. I decided to give it another prompt once it finished; try this for yourself.

Prompt: Please make the five blog post suggestions less severe and tone informal.

ChatGPT:

YES, HERE ARE A FEW MORE JOVIAL AND UNOFFICIAL BLOG POST RECOMMENDATIONS FOR HIGH SEARCH VOLUME AND LOW COMPETITION KEYWORDS FOR PURCHASING A NEW LAPTOP:

THE ARTICLE "HOW TO SCORE A SWEET LAPTOP DEAL WITHOUT SELLING YOUR SOUL TO THE TECH GODS"

THIS ARTICLE COULD PROVIDE ADVICE ON WHERE TO SEEK, HOW TO HAGGLE, AND WHEN TO BUY IN ORDER TO FIND AMAZING LAPTOP PRICES.

THE BOOK "THE ULTIMATE LAPTOP SURVIVAL GUIDE: HOW TO KEEP YOUR LAPTOP ALIVE AND KICKING"

THIS ARTICLE MAY PROVIDE TIPS FOR LAPTOP OWNERS ON HOW TO KEEP THEIR EQUIPMENT OPERATING EFFICIENTLY AND AVOID TYPICAL PROBLEMS LIKE OVERHEATING, BATTERY DRAIN, AND VIRUSES.

THE JOURNEY OF TRIAL AND ERROR THAT IS "THE SEARCH FOR THE PERFECT LAPTOP"

THE SELECTION OF THE IDEAL LAPTOP CAN BE MADE HUMOROUSLY IN THIS POST BY INCLUDING PERSONAL ANECDOTES AND SUGGESTIONS FOR VARIOUS USER TYPES (SUCH AS GAMERS, PROFESSIONALS, AND STUDENTS).

IT'S "THE GREAT LAPTOP DEBATE: PC VS. MAC" THIS ARTICLE MIGHT EXAMINE THE BENEFITS AND DRAWBACKS OF SEVERAL LAPTOP BRANDS AND OPERATING SYSTEMS AND PROVIDE GUIDANCE FOR SELECTING THE BEST OPTION FOR YOUR REQUIREMENTS.

THE BOOK "LAPTOP BUYING 101: A CRASH COURSE FOR THE TECH-CHALLENGED"

THIS ARTICLE COULD SERVE AS A BASIC BUYER'S GUIDE FOR LAPTOPS, PROVIDING AN OVERVIEW OF IMPORTANT SPECIFICATIONS AND FEATURES, AN EXPLANATION OF TECHNICAL TERMS, AND ADVICE FOR NAVIGATING THE BEWILDERING WORLD OF LAPTOPS.

You can see the basic idea - you can change the prompt and use it to create a blog for any topic in any style or tone.

If you need more detail or the script generated isn't long enough, you can type another prompt, like "Please rewrite it to be longer with more detail on the processors."

PROMPT: Please rewrite it to be longer with more detail on [topic]

If you are a student or have kids, they can use ChatGPT for homework tutoring. Students can use ChatGPT for several areas of their assignments, including:

Responding to inquiries, problem-solving, conceptual support, and enhancing writing abilities.

PROMPT: I am a student. Can you explain to me some critical concepts in calculus?

ChatGPT:

SURE! CALCULUS IS A BRANCH OF MATHEMATICS THAT DEALS WITH THE STUDY OF RATES OF CHANGE AND THE ACCUMULATION OF SMALL CHANGES. HERE ARE SOME KEY CONCEPTS IN CALCULUS:

LIMITS: THE VALUE THAT A FUNCTION APPROACHES WHEN THE INPUT (THE INDEPENDENT VARIABLE) APPROACHES A SPECIFIC VALUE IS

REFERRED TO AS A LIMIT. CALCULUS LIMITS ARE CRUCIAL BECAUSE THEY ENABLE US TO STUDY HOW FUNCTIONS BEHAVE CLOSE TO SPECIFIC PLACES, EVEN IF THE FUNCTION IS NOT DEFINED THERE.

DERIVATIVES: A DERIVATIVE IS A MEASUREMENT OF THE CHANGE IN A FUNCTION WITH CHANGING INPUT. THE SLOPE OF A FUNCTION AT A GIVEN LOCATION IS THE DERIVATIVE OF THAT FUNCTION. DERIVATIVES ARE USED TO EXAMINE THE BEHAVIOR OF FUNCTIONS, DISCOVER THE MAXIMUM AND LOWEST POINTS OF A FUNCTION, AND RESOLVE OPTIMIZATION ISSUES.

INTEGRALS: DERIVATIVES' OPPOSITE ARE INTEGRALS. THEY TRACK THE ACCUMULATION OF MINUTE CHANGES OVER A PREDETERMINED TIME PERIOD. INTEGRALS CAN BE USED TO COMPUTE THE VOLUME OF A SPHERICAL SHAPE, FIND THE AREA UNDER A CURVE, AND HANDLE ACCUMULATION OR DECAY ISSUES.

THERE ARE A FEW DIFFERENTIATION PRINCIPLES THAT MAKE IT SIMPLER TO LOCATE DERIVATIVES OF PARTICULAR KINDS OF FUNCTIONS. THE POWER RULE, PRODUCT RULE, QUOTIENT RULE, AND CHAIN RULE ARE A FEW EXAMPLES.

FINDING THE MAXIMUM OR MINIMUM VALUE OF A FUNCTION UNDER SPECIFIC RESTRICTIONS IS THE GOAL OF OPTIMIZATION ISSUES. CALCULUS FREQUENTLY INVOLVES ISSUES OF THIS NATURE, WHICH MIGHT INVOLVE A VARIETY OF FUNCTIONS, SUCH AS QUADRATIC, EXPONENTIAL, LINEAR, AND TRIGONOMETRIC FUNCTIONS.

THESE ARE JUST A FEW OF THE KEY CONCEPTS IN CALCULUS, BUT THEY ARE FUNDAMENTAL TO UNDERSTANDING THE SUBJECT. IF YOU HAVE ANY MORE QUESTIONS OR NEED FURTHER CLARIFICATION, FEEL FREE TO ASK!

And, of course, the student can drill down as far as they want or need to get the data and information they need. ChatGPT can help assist and expedite the research process for academic projects, tasks, or personal interests. It can help with various techniques in the research process, including topic choice, background information about the topic, locating appropriate resources, arranging the research, and citation.

PROMPT: I am a student working on a project in calculus. Can you provide me with some creative ideas?

ChatGPT:

OF COURSE! HERE ARE SOME PROJECT IDEAS IN CALCULUS THAT YOU MIGHT FIND INTERESTING:

APPLICATIONS OF DERIVATIVES: PICK A REAL-WORLD EXAMPLE, SUCH AS A ROLLER COASTER'S ROUTE, A BRIDGE'S DESIGN, OR A PARTICLE'S MOTION. CALCULUS CAN BE USED TO STUDY THE SYSTEM'S BEHAVIOR AND PINPOINT KEY CHARACTERISTICS, INCLUDING MAXIMUM AND MINIMUM POINTS, RATES OF CHANGE, AND CONCAVITY.

INVESTIGATE SEVERAL INTEGRATION STRATEGIES, SUCH AS PARTIAL FRACTIONS, PARTS-BASED INTEGRATION, AND SUBSTITUTION-BASED INTEGRATION. EXAMINE HOW THESE METHODS CAN BE APPLIED TO INTEGRALS TO SIMPLIFY THEM AND MAKE THEM SIMPLER TO ANSWER.

FIRST-ORDER AND SECOND-ORDER DIFFERENTIAL EQUATIONS ARE JUST TWO EXAMPLES OF THE MANY FORMS OF DIFFERENTIAL EQUATIONS THAT CAN BE STUDIED. UTILIZE METHODS LIKE VARIABLE SEPARATION AND INTEGRATING FACTORS TO ANALYZE HOW THESE EQUATIONS BEHAVE.

INVESTIGATE OPTIMIZATION ISSUES INVOLVING A VARIETY OF FUNCTIONS, INCLUDING LINEAR, QUADRATIC, EXPONENTIAL, AND TRIGONOMETRIC FUNCTIONS. UTILIZE CALCULUS TO SOLVE THESE ISSUES, THEN ANALYZE THE SOLUTIONS IN LIGHT OF THE ISSUE AT HAND.

FRACTALS ARE INTRICATE GEOMETRIC PATTERNS THAT REPEAT THEMSELVES AT VARIOUS SCALES. LEARN ABOUT FRACTAL GEOMETRY. CALCULUS CAN BE USED TO EXAMINE THE CHARACTERISTICS OF FRACTALS AND LOOK AT HOW THEY ARE USED IN AREAS LIKE COMPUTER GRAPHICS, PHYSICS, AND BIOLOGY.

SELECT A FAMILY OF FUNCTIONS FOR YOUR GRAPHICAL ANALYSIS, SUCH AS POLYNOMIALS, EXPONENTIALS, OR TRIGONOMETRIC FUNCTIONS. USE CALCULUS TO ANALYZE THE GRAPHS OF THESE FUNCTIONS BY IDENTIFYING CRITICAL POINTS, INFLECTION POINTS, AND ASYMPTOTES.

I HOPE THESE IDEAS INSPIRE YOU AND HELP YOU COME UP WITH A GREAT PROJECT IN CALCULUS!

How about help with learning a language? To help students practice and advance their language skills, ChatGPT provides translations, grammar explanations, vocabulary drills, and conversation simulations. Students may also benefit from planning a program to increase their language abilities.

PROMPT: I am an intermediate-level Spanish speaker and want to improve my skills. Can you offer me a weekly schedule to improve my Spanish?

ChatGPT:

OF COURSE! HERE IS A WEEKLY SCHEDULE THAT YOU CAN FOLLOW TO IMPROVE YOUR SPANISH SKILLS:

MONDAY:

START THE DAY BY READING A SPANISH NEWS ARTICLE OR A SHORT STORY.

THIS WILL HELP YOU IMPROVE YOUR READING COMPREHENSION AND EXPAND YOUR VOCABULARY.

WATCH A SPANISH TV SHOW OR MOVIE. YOU CAN USE SUBTITLES IF NECESSARY BUT TRY TO FOCUS ON LISTENING TO THE SPOKEN LANGUAGE AND UNDERSTANDING THE CONTEXT OF THE DIALOGUE. SPEND 30 MINUTES PRACTICING VERB CONJUGATION. CHOOSE A FEW VERBS AND PRACTICE CONJUGATING THEM IN DIFFERENT TENSES AND MOODS. THIS WILL HELP YOU IMPROVE YOUR GRAMMAR SKILLS AND BECOME MORE COMFORTABLE USING DIFFERENT VERB FORMS.

TUESDAY:

START THE DAY BY LISTENING TO A SPANISH PODCAST. THIS WILL HELP YOU IMPROVE YOUR LISTENING SKILLS AND EXPOSE YOU TO DIFFERENT ACCENTS AND DIALECTS.

READ A FEW PAGES FROM A SPANISH NOVEL OR A NON-FICTION BOOK. THIS WILL HELP YOU IMPROVE YOUR READING SPEED AND COMPREHENSION. SPEND 30 MINUTES PRACTICING SPANISH CONVERSATION. FIND A LANGUAGE EXCHANGE PARTNER OR JOIN A LANGUAGE LEARNING GROUP AND PRACTICE SPEAKING SPANISH WITH SOMEONE ELSE.

WEDNESDAY:

START THE DAY BY WATCHING A SPANISH TUTORIAL VIDEO ON A TOPIC THAT INTERESTS YOU. THIS WILL HELP YOU LEARN NEW VOCABULARY AND TECHNICAL TERMS RELATED TO YOUR FIELD OF INTEREST. SPEND SOME TIME WRITING IN SPANISH. YOU CAN WRITE A DIARY ENTRY, A SHORT STORY, OR A BLOG POST. THIS WILL HELP YOU IMPROVE YOUR WRITING SKILLS AND BECOME MORE COMFORTABLE EXPRESSING YOURSELF IN SPANISH. SPEND 30 MINUTES PRACTICING GRAMMAR EXERCISES. CHOOSE A GRAMMAR TOPIC THAT YOU FIND CHALLENGING, SUCH AS THE SUBJUNCTIVE MOOD OR THE USE OF PREPOSITIONS, AND PRACTICE EXERCISES TO REINFORCE YOUR UNDERSTANDING.

THURSDAY:

START THE DAY LISTENING TO A SPANISH SONG AND TRYING TO UNDERSTAND

THE LYRICS. THIS WILL HELP YOU IMPROVE YOUR LISTENING SKILLS AND EXPOSE YOU TO DIFFERENT GENRES OF MUSIC. SPEND SOME TIME READING SPANISH BLOGS OR SOCIAL MEDIA POSTS. THIS WILL HELP YOU IMPROVE YOUR READING COMPREHENSION AND BECOME MORE FAMILIAR WITH COLLOQUIAL EXPRESSIONS AND SLANG. SPEND 30 MINUTES PRACTICING VOCABULARY. CHOOSE A THEME, SUCH AS FOOD, TRAVEL, OR TECHNOLOGY, AND PRACTICE LEARNING NEW VOCABULARY RELATED TO THAT THEME.

FRIDAY:

START THE DAY BY WATCHING A SPANISH DOCUMENTARY OR A NEWS PROGRAM. THIS WILL HELP YOU IMPROVE YOUR LISTENING AND COMPREHENSION SKILLS AND EXPOSE YOU TO CURRENT EVENTS IN THE SPANISH-SPEAKING WORLD. PRACTICE SPEAKING SPANISH WITH A TUTOR OR A LANGUAGE TEACHER. GET FEEDBACK ON YOUR PRONUNCIATION, GRAMMAR, AND FLUENCY. SPEND SOME TIME REVIEWING WHAT YOU HAVE LEARNED DURING THE WEEK. MAKE A LIST OF NEW WORDS, EXPRESSIONS, AND GRAMMAR CONCEPTS THAT YOU HAVE LEARNED, AND PRACTICE USING THEM IN CONTEXT.

I HOPE THIS SCHEDULE HELPS YOU IMPROVE YOUR SPANISH SKILLS AND BECOME MORE CONFIDENT USING THE LANGUAGE!

Let's turn our focus back to business and ways to make money online. Let's start with applications for SEO and marketing. And specifically on creating content for campaigns with content marketing. Beyond just generating business ideas, AI-generated texts can be used in marketing for various reasons, such as content development for content marketing, including emails, social media postings, and blog pieces. Need help writing scripts and telling stories to convey ideas to market products and services?

PROMPT: Generate advertising for a new electric golf cart

ChatGPT:

INTRODUCING OUR BRAND-NEW ELECTRIC GOLF CART, THE NEWEST IMPROVEMENT TO YOUR GOLFING EXPERIENCE!

OUR GOLF CART IS THE IDEAL PARTNER FOR YOUR UPCOMING ROUND OF GOLF THANKS TO ITS STYLISH APPEARANCE, COZY SEATS, AND STRONG ELECTRIC MOTOR. EMBRACE THE FUTURE OF GOLF TECHNOLOGY AND BID ADIEU TO THE BOTHER OF GAS-POWERED CARTS.

WITH THE SMOOTH AND QUIET RIDE OF OUR ELECTRIC GOLF CART, YOU CAN CONCENTRATE ON YOUR GAME WITHOUT ANY OUTSIDE INTERRUPTIONS. IT ALSO LEAVES NO EMISSIONS, WHICH LESSENS YOUR CARBON FOOTPRINT ON THE GOLF FIELD.

WE ALSO HAVE CUTTING-EDGE TECHNOLOGY IN OUR GOLF CART, SUCH AS A TOUCHSCREEN DISPLAY, GPS NAVIGATION, AND BLUETOOTH CONNECTIVITY. PLAY A RELAXED ROUND OF GOLF WHILE STAYING IN TOUCH WITH YOUR FRIENDS AND FAMILY.

OUR ELECTRIC GOLF CART IS SIMPLE TO MANEUVER ON ANY SURFACE, WHETHER YOU'RE PLAYING ON A LEVEL COURSE OR A MOUNTAINOUS ONE, THANKS TO ITS LIGHTWEIGHT AND COMPACT DESIGN. FURTHERMORE, YOU WON'T HAVE TO WORRY ABOUT RUNNING OUT OF POWER IN THE MIDDLE OF A GAME THANKS TO ITS LONG-LASTING BATTERY.

TRY OUR BRAND-NEW ELECTRIC GOLF CART TODAY TO IMPROVE YOUR GOLFING EXPERIENCE. YOU WON'T REGRET IT, WE PROMISE.

ChatGPT may produce customized content for clients by utilizing its natural language processing capabilities and considering their preferences, previous behavior, and demographics. This allows companies to provide targeted content that engages with customers more personally, increasing engagement and conversion rates.

Audience research entails gathering data and insights about that group to understand better the interests, tastes, habits, and needs of the target audience. This aids businesses in more efficient marketing.

You can discover new methods and approaches for utilizing ChatGPT successfully by working with people who are also knowledgeable about the program. You can fully use ChatGPT's capabilities and produce better results in your activities and projects by adhering to these strategies and continually working to increase your ChatGPT expertise. ChatGPT can be used to examine client information like internet searches and Facebook interactions to write product descriptions to create patterns and trends in consumer behavior based on past purchases.

A key marketing component is providing potential buyers with information about a product's qualities, advantages, and value through product descriptions. , ChatGPT can help create product descriptions that appeal to the interests and preferences of the target audience.

CHAPTER 9

The Best Prompts for ChatGPT Monetization

This chapter provides some "act as" examples for ChatGPT online revenue generation. ChatGPT can offer tailored coaching sessions to assist clients in achieving their objectives and overcoming obstacles. This service can be paid for either per session or through a subscription model.

Top-notch explanations, crystal-clear communication, and straightforward language are all strengths of ChatGPT. ChatGPT's simplification of complicated concepts makes it easier for users to understand concepts outside of their area of expertise and without the need for prior technical terminology knowledge, according to an explanation of blockchain that an 11-year-old can understand.

PROMPT: I want to learn about (insert specific topic). Explain (insert topic) in simple terms. Please explain to me like I'm 15 years old.

ChatGPT can help with language acquisition, conversation practice, and grammar and pronunciation correction. Both subscription and per-lesson fees are options for making money from this business. ChatGPT provides expert budgeting, financial planning, and investment advice. This service can create considerable revenues with a subscription fee or a percentage of assets under control. ChatGPT can help you reach your objectives with customized diet and exercise regimens, wellness recommendations, and mental health assistance. Subscribe or pay per session.

ChatGPT advises on furniture placement, color schemes, and innovation to make your room a masterpiece. Subscription or per-project payment? ChatGPT lets you create a fascinating, professional resume that attracts employers. ChatGPT can help prospective writers with story, character, and editing as creative writing instructors.

Discover unlimited blog posts, social media, and other content ideas to engage your audience. As a content marketer, use ChatGPT's creative platform to produce new and exciting ideas to reach your goals. ChatGPT eliminates writer's block and inspires creativity. With this tool, create engaging, informational content that resonates with your audience. I have a lot of content from over a decade of blogging. ChatGPT is one of my favorite tools for easy organization and management. This book will help you write compelling beginnings, redesign specific sections, generate engaging gags and hooks, and write useful FAQs for your blog's key topics.

As a talented content producer, you must guarantee that your material lasts and resonates. Never create underperforming evergreen content. Simple but effective changes can maximize content potential. As a freelancer, I provide high-quality material updates and cleanup for blogs, websites, and other digital platforms. ChatGPT will turn your messy disaster into a clean, digestible masterpiece. A refined display replaces the difficulty of understanding jumbled data. Give it the text to edit. I need content to finish this. Give it the text to rewrite.

ChatGPT makes scheduling, emailing, and file organization easy. Our platform is a virtual assistant for time-pressed professionals. Focus on critical tasks to boost productivity and save time. ChatGPT can help you write engaging headlines, taglines, and other copy. This effective copywriting tool can enhance conversions and sales.

ChatGPT provides seamless customer service! ChatGPT can quickly answer frequently asked inquiries regarding products, shipping, and returns. Customer service without the wait is here now with ChatGPT. Serving customers fast and efficiently frees up time for other tasks. This sophisticated tool can generate leads, send personalized follow-up emails, and provide clients with customized recommendations. ChatGPT lets you sell for your organization by providing excellent customer experiences that convert. ChatGPT can transform your business—try it today! This simple method boosts customer revenue and sales.

ChatGPT is your market research tool for market trends, customer behavior, and competitor action. Gather and analyze data to stay ahead by making informed judgments. ChatGPT can help you discover market trends and consumer preferences to make business decisions confidently. Improve client insights.

Unlock your imagination and discover the unlimited story, narrative, and aesthetic possibilities with ChatGPT. I'll gladly assist you! As a creative writer, you can now aim to capture your brand's character and personality and develop engaging content for your target audience. ChatGPT will collaborate with you to write website copy, product descriptions, social media postings, and other on-brand and on-message content. Tell it about your business and goals, and let's start making great content!

ChatGPT simulates employment interviews. Inform ChatGPT about your planned job application. ChatGPT provides an interview-like experience with relevant and appropriate questions.

Provide exceptional services to clients across industries to maximize your earnings. ChatGPT lets you easily portray different professionals and meet clients' needs. Today, monetize your skills! Use ChatGPT to start a successful business. For over 3,000 prompts, please click the link on the first page of this book, but here is a list of 20 PROMTS based on what activity you need to accomplish.

- Automate email: "Generate a polite response to this email about scheduling a meeting."

- Draft reports: "Create a summary report of these sales data."

- Write code: "Write a Python script to automate data entry."

- Generate content: "Write a blog post about the benefits of time management."

- Create presentations: "Design a PowerPoint presentation on AI advancements."

- Plan events: "Outline a plan for a corporate team-building event."

- Brainstorm ideas: "Generate ten innovative ideas for a new mobile app."

- Write proposals: "Draft a proposal for a new marketing strategy."

- Automate social media: "Create a week's worth of social media posts for a fitness brand."

- Write business plans: "Write an executive summary for a tech startup business plan."

- Create lesson plans: "Design a lesson plan for teaching Python programming to beginners."

- Write resumes and cover letters: "Draft a cover letter for a software engineer position."

- Generate marketing copy: "Write a catchy product description for a new smartphone."

- Write research summaries: "Summarize this research paper on climate change."

- Generate recipes: "Create a healthy recipe using these ingredients: chicken, broccoli, quinoa."

- Product reviews: "Write a review for the latest iPhone model."

- Create workout plans: "Design a 4-week workout plan for weight loss."

- Write newsletters: "Draft a monthly newsletter for a local book club."

- Create meeting agendas: "Generate an agenda for a project status update meeting."

- Write press releases: "Draft a press release for a new product launch."

You can also use ChatGPT Prompts to come up with original content ideas. For example, if you need help getting popular using AI tools – we can help you quickly develop original content ideas utilizing ChatGPT.

PROMPT: Come up with unique and innovative content ideas that are unconventional for {the topic}

Use ChatGPT to test your understanding and learn about a topic, subject, or business.

PROMPT: Give me a short quiz that teaches me [what you want to learn]

Using it to develop your decision-making or managerial skills would be best.

PROMPT: I am trying to decide if I should [insert decision]. Please give me a list of good and bad that will help me decide why I should or shouldn't make this decision.

And while you are in a role, why not get out of your comfort zone and get criticized by ChatGPT?

PROMPT: I want you to act as a critic. Criticize the information above and convince me why they are bad.

And if you are stuck coming up with a great new prompt, be creative and request that ChatGPT create prompts for you.

PROMPT: I am a [insert your profession]. Generate a list of the most powerful prompts to help someone {my profession} get more done and save time.

The above was pivotal in my success, and I recommend getting very good with prompts. The next idea is a simple method that creates prompts for any situation or subject. Act in the role of [Profession], you will consider this criterion [pertinent to profession] and produce a customized product in response to my request. My initial demand is for you to ["Enter your request"]

Here is a small sample list of potential professionals, salespersons, productivity coaches, financiers, consultants, virtual assistants, social media manager coaches for public speaking, content creator, tutor, technology specialist, coaches for self-improvement, fitness professional, career counselor, resume author, nutritionist, web designer, and app developer. PROMPT:

- ACT AS A CONSULTANT: USE YOUR DOMAIN KNOWLEDGE TO OFFER CLIENTS GUIDANCE AND CONSULTATION SERVICES FOR {TOPIC OR REQUEST}

- ACT AS A FREELANCER: TO DO NUMEROUS JOBS FOR CLIENTS, OFFER YOUR SKILLS AS A FREELANCER ON WEBSITES LIKE FIVERR OR UPWORK.

- ACT AS AN AFFILIATE MARKETER: EARN MONEY BY PROMOTING THE GOODS OR SERVICES OF OTHER PEOPLE IN EXCHANGE FOR A COMMISSION ON EACH LEAD OR SALE THAT COMES FROM YOUR SPECIAL AFFILIATE LINK.

- ACT AS A SOCIAL MEDIA INFLUENCE: UTILIZE YOUR SOCIAL MEDIA FOLLOWING TO PROMOTE BRANDS' GOODS AND SERVICES TO YOUR AUDIENCE BY TAKING ON THE ROLE OF A SOCIAL MEDIA INFLUENCER.

- ACT AS AN ONLINE TUTOR: TUTOR STUDENTS ONLINE BY SHARING YOUR KNOWLEDGE AND EXPERIENCE IN A PARTICULAR SUBJECT AREA THROUGH WEBSITES, CHEGG, OR TUTORME.

- ACT AS A CONTENT CREATOR: USE PLATFORMS LIKE YOUTUBE, TIKTOK, OR INSTAGRAM TO CREATE INTERESTING AND EDUCATIONAL MATERIAL THAT DRAWS A SIZABLE AUDIENCE AND BRINGS IN MONEY FROM SPONSORSHIPS OR ADVERTISING.

- ACT AS A VIRTUAL ASSISTANT: PROVIDING CLIENTS WITH REMOTE ADMINISTRATIVE AND ORGANIZATIONAL SUPPORT.

- ACT AS A DROPSHIPPER: USE DROPSHIPPING TO SELL THINGS ONLINE WITHOUT KEEPING INVENTORY BY COLLABORATING WITH DISTRIBUTORS OR MANUFACTURERS.

These are just a few illustrations of how "act as" suggestions might be used to generate online income. The key is finding a means to monetize your talents, passions, and interests through numerous online outlets.

CHAPTER 10

Beyond ChatGPT And 100 New Ai Tools

In this Chapter, I will remind you how powerful ChatGPT is, but I also want to share with you what Beyond ChatGPT is. So many new AI Tools work with ChatGPT, and there are already a few competitors. Learning to work with other AI tools and knowing when to use other platforms will be valuable.

Artificial Intelligence is a field of computer science that focuses on developing programs and algorithms, which are step-by-step processes designed to solve problems or answer questions. The aim is to create machines that can operate in a more human-like manner.

There exist various subfields within this scientific discipline, which include:

Natural Language Processing (NLP) is a field of study that aims to create seamless communication between humans and computers. Specialized software facilitates natural language processing, enabling machines to comprehend human language, generate coherent language, and engage with humans through language.

Machine learning (ML) prioritizes a machine's capacity to analyze and utilize information to provide recommendations or make decisions based on the given data sets.

Computer vision pertains to developing machines capable of comprehending and interpreting visual data. Robotics technology is capable of autonomous physical task execution, including human interaction, without constant human supervision. Discover the immense benefits of mastering ChatGPT, unlocking its advanced features, and creating a sustainable source of passive income with my comprehensive guide. Discover the thorough analysis of ChatGPT's boundaries and the ultimate winning tactics.

No matter what your goals may be - launching a new business, expanding an existing one, or boosting your income as a freelancer, entrepreneur, or employee - ChatGPT has got you covered. We've provided many examples and expert advice on how our platform can assist you in achieving success.

Discover the power of repurposing content across multiple social media channels for maximum impact. Discover how to create passive revenue streams from the ground up! We've covered you, from ideation and research to developing a basic structure, producing content, and marketing via email and social media.

Discover the critical takeaway from this book: ChatGPT's remarkable ability to create fantastic content and generate lucrative passive income streams online. Discover the importance of acknowledging that ChatGPT has boundaries and cannot replace the finesse of human editing.

Achieving success with ChatGPT is contingent upon strictly following the recommended best practices outlined in this book. Achieving your desired outcomes requires a strategic approach. This involves setting clear and measurable goals, conducting thorough research, refining your prompts to elicit optimal responses, and dedicating ample time to editing and enhancing your content.

Unlock the full potential of ChatGPT by strategically selecting your desired income streams and establishing clear, achievable, and quantifiable objectives. Maximize your results by dedicating time to perfecting your prompts. Discover the most effective prompts by experimenting with different options and keeping track of their outcomes. While ChatGPT delivers top-notch content, it has imperfections. Take the time to meticulously edit and refine the generated content to ensure it meets your exact requirements and is completely error-free.

Discover the world of ChatGPT and its vast array of applications with this all-encompassing beginner's guidebook. Discover the essential building blocks of ChatGPT, delve into its intricate technicalities, and unlock its limitless potential for diverse applications. With its remarkable ability to produce responses strikingly like a human's, ChatGPT is the ultimate solution for diverse prompts and inquiries. Experience the exceptional advantage of ChatGPT's coherent and contextually appropriate responses to natural language inputs. This versatile tool is invaluable for conversational AI applications like chatbots and personal assistants. Unlock a world of possibilities with the ability to perform tasks like text summarization, trivia question answering, and image natural language description.

Discover the limitless potential of ChatGPT! Our cutting-edge technology extends far beyond mere text generation. Experience the versatility and power of this advanced tool that has the potential to revolutionize the world of natural language processing and artificial intelligence.

Unlock the full potential of this cutting-edge technology by harnessing its power with ample computational resources and expert know-how. Experience advanced conversational AI and natural language processing with ChatGPT - a significant advancement in the field. With its proven track record in healthcare, customer service, and research, this versatile technology boasts a wide range of capabilities and limitless potential for various industries.

ChatGPT is a powerful AI model that has revolutionized natural language processing. It can generate human-like responses to various inputs, making it useful for various applications, including customer service, education, and entertainment. However, ChatGPT, like any other technology, has limitations and challenges that must be overcome, such as bias, context understanding, and user trust. To fully realize ChatGPT's potential, it is critical to continue developing and refining the model while ensuring it is used ethically and responsibly.

We can use ChatGPT to improve our lives and create a better future. ChatGPT aims to enhance communication between humans and machines and provide users with a more personalized and engaging experience. It can transform industries and open new opportunities for businesses and individuals. ChatGPT, however, has limitations and challenges, including potential biases, context understanding, and user trust.

These issues must be addressed to ensure ChatGPT is used ethically and responsibly.

ChatGPT represents a significant advancement in artificial intelligence and natural language processing, and it has the potential to drive future innovation and progress. As an OpenAI product/service, ChatGPT does not have a direct monetization strategy as an AI language model. On the other hand, businesses and organizations can use ChatGPT skills to generate revenue in various ways.

While ChatGPT has been the primary focus throughout this book, it's worth noting the abundance of new tools emerging monthly, with hundreds being introduced regularly. Discover what lies Beyond ChatGPT in this exciting new chapter. Discover cutting-edge AI technology that rivals ChatGPT. Discover powerful AI tools and agents that seamlessly integrate with ChatGPT to elevate, refine, and expedite your ChatGPT experience.

PROMPT: give me a list of the stocks that could 10x next bull run.

CHATGPT:

AS AN AI DEVELOPED BY OPENAI, I MUST CLARIFY THAT I'M NOT ABLE TO PROVIDE SPECIFIC STOCK PREDICTIONS OR INVESTMENT ADVICE, AS THIS REQUIRES AN UNDERSTANDING OF REAL-TIME MARKET CONDITIONS, INDIVIDUAL COMPANY PERFORMANCES, AND OTHER VARIABLES, WHICH I DON'T HAVE.

AS OF MY TRAINING CUT-OFF IN SEPTEMBER 2021, I CAN PROVIDE GENERAL ADVICE ON HOW TO IDENTIFY POTENTIALLY HIGH-GROWTH STOCKS:

1. EMERGING INDUSTRIES: COMPANIES OPERATING IN INDUSTRIES THAT ARE POISED FOR SIGNIFICANT GROWTH, SUCH AS RENEWABLE ENERGY, ARTIFICIAL INTELLIGENCE, BLOCKCHAIN TECHNOLOGY, AND BIOTECH.

2. INNOVATION: COMPANIES THAT ARE LEADERS IN INNOVATION, HAVE A UNIQUE PRODUCT OR SERVICE, OR ARE DISRUPTING EXISTING INDUSTRIES.

3. FINANCIAL HEALTH: COMPANIES WITH STRONG BALANCE SHEETS, GOOD CASH FLOW, AND MANAGEABLE DEBT.

4. STRONG MANAGEMENT: LEADERSHIP WITH A PROVEN TRACK SUCCESS RECORD CAN BE A GOOD INDICATOR OF A COMPANY'S POTENTIAL FOR GROWTH.

5. MARKET POTENTIAL: COMPANIES TARGETING LARGE AND GROWING MARKETS.

6. COMPETITIVE ADVANTAGE: COMPANIES WITH A SUSTAINABLE COMPETITIVE ADVANTAGE SUCH AS PROPRIETARY TECHNOLOGY, STRONG BRAND, OR COST ADVANTAGES.

PLEASE CONSULT WITH A FINANCIAL ADVISOR OR CONDUCT THOROUGH DUE DILIGENCE BEFORE MAKING INVESTMENT DECISIONS.

So, it didn't want to give me a list and remember the data is not current, so it can be very hard to get it to help predict current events based on the recent past, but I pushed with more prompts, and here is what I got

ChatGPT:

- TESLA INC. (TSLA): A LEADER IN THE ELECTRIC VEHICLE MARKET.

- MODERNA INC. (MRNA): A KEY PLAYER IN THE DEVELOPMENT OF MRNA TECHNOLOGY FOR VACCINES.

- AMAZON.COM INC. (AMZN): CONTINUOUSLY INNOVATING IN E-COMMERCE, CLOUD COMPUTING, AND OTHER TECH DOMAINS.

- ALPHABET INC. (GOOGL): THE PARENT COMPANY OF GOOGLE, KNOWN FOR ITS INNOVATIVE TECHNOLOGIES IN VARIOUS FIELDS LIKE SEARCH, CLOUD COMPUTING, AI, AND MORE.

- MICROSOFT CORPORATION (MSFT): A TECH COMPANY WITH STRONG FINANCIALS AND A WIDE RANGE OF SUCCESSFUL PRODUCTS.

- APPLE INC. (AAPL): KNOWN FOR ITS ROBUST FINANCIAL HEALTH AND POPULAR PRODUCTS.

- BERKSHIRE HATHAWAY INC. (BRK.A): LED BY WARREN BUFFETT, KNOWN FOR HIS LONG-TERM INVESTMENT PHILOSOPHY.

- JPMORGAN CHASE & CO. (JPM): LED BY JAMIE DIMON, REGARDED AS A STRONG LEADER IN THE FINANCE INDUSTRY.

- NVIDIA CORPORATION (NVDA): A LEADING COMPANY IN THE GPU MARKET WITH GROWING APPLICATIONS IN AI, GAMING, AND DATA CENTERS.

- ADOBE INC. (ADBE): PROVIDING SOFTWARE SOLUTIONS WITH A SIGNIFICANT MARKET TO CATER TO.

- THE COCA-COLA COMPANY (KO): WITH A STRONG BRAND NAME AND WORLDWIDE PRESENCE, IT'S A LEADER IN THE BEVERAGE INDUSTRY.

- JOHNSON & JOHNSON (JNJ): A DIVERSIFIED HEALTHCARE COMPANY WITH A BROAD RANGE OF WELL-ESTABLISHED PRODUCTS.

So, you can see how powerful this tool will continue to be, especially as it gets current data and events. But as we mentioned at the beginning of

this chapter, there is some new coopetition in the AI space.

Perplexity AI can be the ultimate chatbot ready to take on any challenge! ChatGPT

Step into the world of digital AI, where AI chatbots gather and mingle. Meet Perplexity AI, the scrappy newcomer ready to take on the reigning champ, ChatGPT, and shake up the entire AI landscape. This up-and-comer aims to leave the competition in the dust by boasting an impressive lineage, a vast array of features, and a top-notch mobile app. https://www.perplexity.ai

So, I asked Perplexity the same question I asked ChatGPT and got a very different response to the first prompt, as Perplexity uses a different method of answering questions.

PROMPT: give me a list of the stocks that could 10x next bull run.

Perplexity:

HERE ARE SOME STOCKS THAT COULD POTENTIALLY 10X IN THE NEXT BULL RUN, ACCORDING TO THE SEARCH RESULTS:

1.   ROCKET LAB

2.   LANZATECH GLOBAL, NIO, AND JOBY AVIATION

3.   DESKTOP METAL, GINKGO BIOWORKS, SOFI, REAL REAL

4. DERMTECH, DMY TECHNOLOGY GROUP II, SNAP, SQUARE, SOFI VIA CHAMATH PALIHAPITIYA'S IPOE

5. NVDA, DICK'S SPORTING GOODS, PERFICIENT, MODERN

6. CRYPTOCURRENCIES SUCH AS ETHEREUM AND DOGECOIN

IT'S IMPORTANT TO NOTE THAT INVESTING IN SPECULATIVE STOCKS OR CRYPTOCURRENCIES CAN BE RISKY AND SHOULD BE DONE WITH CAUTION. IT'S ALWAYS A GOOD IDEA TO DO YOUR RESEARCH AND CONSULT WITH A FINANCIAL ADVISOR BEFORE MAKING ANY INVESTMENT DECISIONS.

Introducing AgentGPT - the ultimate solution for configuring and deploying autonomous AI agents seamlessly integrating with ChatGPT. Experience the power of cutting-edge technology and take your chatbot game to the next level with AgentGPT. With just a prompt, this incredible tool accomplished in mere minutes what would have taken ten long weeks to achieve solo or two weeks with the assistance of ChatGPT. Imagine having the expertise of a seasoned ChatGPT user at your fingertips with AgentGPT. With the power to select the top 100 prompts for optimal results, you'll be able to streamline your interactions like never before. AgentGPT. It will attempt to reach the goal by thinking of tasks to do, executing them, and learning from the results. https://agentgpt.reworkd.ai

As you will see, when you go to AgentGPT and type in any prompt by clicking Deploy Agent, you will see how it works and thinks. It will develop a Goal and a plan, then execute the tasks needed to reach the goal. It will conduct a market analysis. It will search the web and analyze financial and growth potential, tackling this question like a human but much faster.

These new platforms use a different methodology but deliver similar answers to ChatGPT as it uses the underlying OpenAI API to get its answers.

Another interesting player will be AutoGPT. Discover the limitless possibilities with Auto-GPT, an innovative open-source project. With its advanced framework, Auto-GPT empowers the model to reason and act independently, effortlessly completing various tasks. Experience the future of AI today with AutoGPT. It is only available with the API and for those technical people who can grab the code from GitHub and integrate the platform.

Discover the undeniable truth: Not all lists are created equal regarding ChatGPT competitors. With three distinct rankings at your fingertips, it's imperative to hone your discerning skills and never settle for the initial response. As I keep mentioning, verify everything often. You can google ChatGPT agents and get a list that today includes Auto-GPT, BabyAGI, AgentGPT, Microsoft's Jarvis, ChaosGPT, and others. Jarvis is A collaborative system with an LLM (Large Language Model) as the controller and numerous expert models as collaborative executors.

Hugging Face is the best new community and data science platform. It has cutting-edge tools that make it easy to design, train, and deploy ML (machine language) models using open-source code and technology. Hugging Face offers data science's future now. It is such a supportive environment to collaborate on open-source projects. With cutting-edge tools, data science teams, specialists, and enthusiasts may collaborate smoothly from anywhere. These technologies are vital as hybrid and flexible working styles become the norm. AI's full potential requires collaboration and a community, as tech giants need help to handle this. A communal "Hub" is provided by Hugging Face. In one place, find and collaborate on cutting-edge models and datasets to help curate the largest datasets and models to democratize AI. Join them with me in democratizing AI. https://huggingface.co

This solution delivers daily updates on the latest and greatest cryptocurrency projects by leveraging an API and crafting custom code. Stay ahead of the game with this powerful tool at your fingertips. Discover the endless possibilities of AgentGPT for enhancing your personal and professional endeavors.

ChatGPT's excellent responses and thorough attention to detail will enhance your interactions! We encourage researching all possibilities, but ChatGPT is the best, especially with its upcoming release. Find the best option for your unique needs. Your needs and tastes will determine the best option. Discover AI's benefits. AI tools can enhance operations, analyze data, and predict results by identifying patterns and trends easily, helping you to become productive and accurate. Use AI to improve data analysis. Modern chatbot technology makes accessing a wealth of information from multiple sources easy. They easily remember and retrieve information, so every detail is noticed. Use succinct questions to maximize inquiry. Use our cutting-edge artificial intelligence tool to pinpoint critical locations with pinpoint accuracy. Get information suited to your needs. Our cutting-edge artificial intelligence technology improves data processing, searches, and selection. Specificity is key to getting correct answers. Modern artificial intelligence applications can sort through Google, Wikipedia, and other digital libraries to boost productivity. This powerful solution boosts productivity and resource efficiency.

Tailor learning at your speed and maximize your potential. Self-paced learning opens up a world of possibilities. Our innovative technology allows fast data processing and learning, maximizing its potential. Understand your cognitive type to improve. Due to poorer visual processing, working memory, or attention regulation, some people need more time to scrutinize the details. Examine how traditional classrooms may limit efficiency and fairness. AI technologies and platforms can enhance your self-directed learning. Customized instruction has advantages! Develop a personalized learning approach to maximize potential and success.

Explore how AI can evaluate your performance and provide immediate feedback. State-of-the-art resources help you achieve your goals for higher education. This efficient strategy lets teachers focus on more important topics. Our cutting-edge technology streamlines the grading process like never before. Master self-learning and AI flaw detection. Verify your writing to ensure accuracy. Use ChatGPT's AI features to get great advice and responses. Discover your full potential by hiring a personal instructor. New AI methods enable more accurate error detection. Verifying information seamlessly improves essay writing. Automate grammatical corrections with AI. Our students always provide accurate work. Teachers are spending less time grading pupils' work.

AI tools can streamline your schooling. Eliminate tedious tasks and boost student and educator productivity. AI apps help with everything from information gathering to assessments. Our cutting-edge technology creates a virtual classroom with virtual instructors for an unmatched learning experience. Our innovative solution lets you learn from multiple sources. Find out how these technologies perform in unusual situations. Explore AI-powered speech-recognition tools. These unique solutions are perfect for anyone with physical or age-related writing and typing challenges. Use voice commands to navigate documents. Accessible schools need this feature.

Here is a list of more than 100 new AI Tools to help you make even more money online with ChatGPT and AI.

1. https://theresanaiforthat.com. The Best site for anyone reading this book today. This has almost 5,000 AI's, so you can find most of the tools below at this site and many more.

2. https://godmode.space Godmode is a web platform to access the powers of AutoGPT and BabyAGI. AI agents are still in their infancy, but they are quickly growing in capabilities, and we hope that Godmode will enable more people to tap into autonomous AI agents even in this early stage. Auto-GPT and BabyAGI inspire Godmode and support GPT-3.5 & GPT-4.

3. https://learningstudioai.com The next-generation online course creation tool

4. https://www.uimagic.io Unlock the future of website design with the power of AI-driven User Interface technology for text-to-web designing.

5. https://venturusai.com Turn your business idea into reality. Generate an analysis of your business idea and give you feedback on how to make it successful.

6. https://text-to-video.vercel.app Text to Video. Create videos with artificial intelligence.

7. https://autogpt.thesamur.ai Chatbot site with ChatGPT models, prompt library, and chat history.

8. https://www.magicslides.app Ideas to Professional Presentations in Seconds. Say bye to boring, laborious presentation-making. Let the computer do the hard work and make the presentations for you!

9. https://agentgpt.reworkd.ai Assemble, configure, and deploy autonomous AI Agents in your browser and let your computer do all the heavy lifting.

10. https://scisummary.com Use AI to summarize scientific articles in seconds. Get 5x research done without constantly disrupting your work.

11. https://seocontent.ai/ Optimize Your Content Strategy with SEO Content AI. Our AI-driven solution optimizes your content for search engines and improves your online presence with high-quality, long-form content.

12. https://business-generator.vercel.app Tool that helps users generate creative business ideas.

13. https://www.gptinf.com A tool that removes AI content by paraphrasing.

14. https://www.helinaik.com/contentcal Create your monthly content calendar with the help of this AI tool.

15. https://www.sincode.ai Create SEO-optimized and plagiarism-free content for your blogs, ads, emails, & website 10X faster.

16. https://pictory.ai Automatically create short, highly sharable branded videos from your long-form content. Quick, easy & cost-effective.

17. https://write.homes/ The ultimate real estate content creation tool

18. https://www.jasper.ai/. The best overall AI writing assistant, leading the market with its impressive features and quality.

19. https://simplerlist.com A productivity assistant that helps you get things done.

20. https://www.translate.video/1-click publish to all social media platforms and manage global audience in a single place

21. https://murf.ai/ Go from text to speech with a versatile AI voice generator. AI-enabled real people's voices. Make studio-quality voiceovers in minutes. Lifelike AI voices for podcasts, videos, and all your professional presentations

22. https://lovo.ai Realistic AI voices that captivate your audience. LOVO is the go-to AI Voice Generator & Text to Speech platform for thousands of creators, saving 90% of their time and budget.

23. https://www.fineshare.com/finevoice/ AI digital voice solution with an amazing real-time voice changer, studio-quality voice recorder, fast and accurate automatic transcription, and realistic AI voice generator.

24. https://www.hitpaw.com/ is the best AI image enlarger to make pictures less blurry and enlarge images without quality loss.

25. https://jobhuntmode.com An AI Based automated career services platform to help navigate the job hunting process.

26. https://gptprompttuner.com Use AI to Generate ChatGPT prompt iterations and run conversations in parallel.

27. https://anyword.com/ It enables the generation of effective copy for ads, emails, landing pages, and content for different platforms.

28. https://www.tango.us. Tango instantly turns what you know into step-by-step guidance—no videos, meetings, or screen shares required.

29. https://www.cutout.pro leverages the power of artificial intelligence and computer vision to deliver a wide range of products both available for individual use and business application
& workflows to achieve efficiency and creation.

30. https://meetotis.com The all-in-one solution for growing businesses to manage their digital marketing on Facebook, Instagram, Google, TikTok, YouTube, and more. An AI-

driven platform that enables businesses to compete and maximize their return on investment.

31. https://www.flick.social/ Handle copywriting, scheduling, hashtags, and analytics seamlessly with Flick, the AI-powered social marketing platform.

32. https://www.looka.com/ Design your beautiful brand. Use Looka's AI-powered platform to design a logo and build a brand you love.

33. https://www.tutorai.me AI platform that allows users to learn about any topic easily.

34. https://ultrabrainstomer.com/ Productivity tool that helps you create social media posts, product campaigns, speeches, and emails.

35. https://www.neuraltext.com/ AI copywriter, SEO content tool, and keyword research tool.

36. https://blogassistant.co AI blog writing tool on the market, and generate complete, non-detectable articles with outlines and blog content.

37. https://www.hypertype.co AI-powered engine to fetch you the most relevant information from your emails and documents. Real-time.

38. https://h2o.ai. A truly open-source generative AI gives organizations like yours the power to create large language models while maintaining your data integrity.

39. https://isaax.org generate custom content for your business needs, including creating blog posts, summarizing texts, and much more.

40. https://www.heygen.com Create engaging videos 10X faster with AI. Meet HeyGen - The best AI video generation platform for your team.

41. https://icons8.com/lunacy Free design software that keeps your flow with AI tools and built-in graphics.

42. https://www.siteexplainer.com AI-powered web app lets you quickly and accurately summarize any website in just a few seconds.

43. https://www.scholarcy.com The online summarizing tool that provides a way to assess and evaluate the importance of documents quickly,

44. https://www.slidesai.io Create Presentation Slides with AI in seconds. Say goodbye to tedious, manual slide creation. Let the AI write the outline and presentation content for you. With our tool, you can easily create professional, engaging slides from any text in no time.

45. https://gptkit.ai AI text generation detection tool.

46. https://krisp.ai Supercharge your online meetings with Voice Productivity AI. Krisp improves the productivity of online meetings with its AI-powered Voice Clarity and Meeting Assistant.

47. https://www.tidio.com Boost your conversions with automation and AI. Answer questions in real-time, 24/7. And so much more.

48. https://chatgptwriter.ai Write emails & messages, fix grammar mistakes, rephrase text, change the writing tone, summarize text, and much more using ChatGPT AI.

49. https://codeium.com A Free AI-Powered Toolkit for Developers.

50. https://codeamigo.dev An AI-powered coding assistant that helps you learn to code like a developer. Today's developers didn't learn binary before learning Python; why should you learn how to code without the most modern tools?

51. http://Tabnine.com → Coding assistant. AI assistant for software developers. Code faster with whole-line & full-function code completions

52. https://speechify.com/ turn text in any format into natural-sounding speech. Based on the web, the platform can take PDFs, emails, docs, or articles and turn them into audio that can be listened to instead of read.

53. https://www.youtubedigest.app YoutubeDigest is a browser extension that uses ChatGPT AI to summarize YouTube videos. Choose from various summary formats and export as PDF, DOCX, or text. ≅

54. https://merlin.foyer.work AI Assistant is a ChatGPT extension to finish any task on any website in seconds.

Merlin is the easy & better way to use ChatGPT. ChatGPT assistant on all websites

55. https://writepanda.io Chat with your podcast/ Youtube! Now easily generate anything.

56. https://designer.microsoft.com Create Images in no time with an AI Image Generator and Editor from Microsoft.

57. https://www.adcreative.ai Artificial Intelligence powered Ad & Social Creatives. Generate conversion-focused ad creatives and social media post creatives in seconds using Artificial Intelligence. Get better results while saving time.

58. https://www.chatpdf.com Efficiently analyze your documents. From financial and sales reports to project and business proposals, training manuals, and legal contracts, ChatPDF can quickly provide you with the information you need.

59. https://huggingface.co Build, train, and deploy state-of-the-art models powered by the reference open source in machine learning. A platform that provides access to pre-trained models for natural language processing tasks.

60. https://theforgeai.com Build AI-powered Applications without writing a single line of code.

61. https://stratup.ai Stratup.ai goes beyond idea generation by providing practical steps to turn your startup ideas into reality.

62. https://hints.so Revolutionize your workflow with an integrated AI assistant from Hints. Visit our website today to explore all the AI integrations.

63. http://audioread.com Audioread If you have endless read-later articles, documents, etc., you'll love this AI tool. Turn articles, PDFs, emails, etc., into podcasts and listen to them while you exercise, commute, run errands, etc.

64. http://adcopy.ai Adcopy AI, the first AI copy tool built to drive more clicks and conversions for digital advertisers, is here. 1. Unlimited outputs for your campaigns 2. Find winning variations in lightning speed 3. Copy & paste any ad for a new variation in seconds

65. http://interviewprep-ai.com Interview Prep AI Are you tired of the stress and anxiety that comes with preparing for a job interview? Interview Prep Al is your personal Al job interview coach that helps you ace your next interview.

66. https://www.eesel.app easel. Use AI to organize your Google Docs, Notion pages, and other work documents automatically. Organizes it all right in your new tab. Best of all, it is free, doesn't compromise privacy, and you don't need to log in to try it.

67. http://hyperwriteai.com HyperWrite is a personal writing helper that creates material for writing ideas, greatly simplifying the work of writers. HyperWrite created a text-to-image section on its website in addition to the writing aid feature.

68. http://ai.nero.com/image-upscaler Nero AI Use this AI to enlarge, improve and clean up your photos. This tool helps you increase image resolution without losing quality.

69. https://threadvoice.net Yes! You can convert this (or any text) to a voice version. You can listen to or download it via

70. http://Formulabot.com Supercharge Excel and Google Sheets. Revolutionize your data & spreadsheet workflow with AI. Transform your text instructions into formulas and more for free in seconds.

71. https://gptexcel.uk Generate Spreadsheet Formulas with AI. An ideal solution for individuals and businesses looking to streamline their spreadsheet processes.

72. http://Cohesive.so Next-generation AI editor. Create magical   content With the most powerful AI editor. End ChatGPT prompt struggles. Create, refine, edit, and publish seamlessly with Cohesive.

73. https://kaiber.ai. Captivating visuals from images or text. Bring your dreams to life. Tell stories like never before with our advanced AI generation engine

74. http://Airops.com/sidekick AI data apps. Draft, fix, and optimize your SQL queries 10x faster. Write documentation instantly.

75. http://Tripnotes.ai AI travel assistant, where do you want to go today?

76. http://Meetcody.ai AI assistant trained to help you grow your business

77. https://www.getsmartcue.com/ Supercharge conversions with SmartCue - the conversion-focused, no-code demo creation & analytics tool for high-performance Go-To-Market teams

78. https://www.joinmano.ai/. Your shortcut to an easier workday. The best way to use ChatGPT on any website.

79. https://poe.com/. Fast, helpful AI chat! Why use it? - iOs and Android apps - Access Sage, Claude, ChatGPT - Explore and use community bots

80. https://vidyo.ai. Make short videos from long ones instantly. Create social-ready short clips from your long videos with AI

81. https://www.audyo.ai. Delight your audience with human-quality AI voices as easily as typing.

82. https://www.superflows.ai. Reply to emails in 1-click. Blaze through your inbox with email summaries and pre-generated replies written in your voice.

83. http://10web.io → AI website builder AI-Powered WordPress Platform. Generate your website in minutes with AI. Get the fastest hosting powered by Google Cloud. Boost your website's PageSpeed score to 90+

84. http://Franks.ai → AI search engine for Business. AI assistant. I can help you find any information and help you write, summarize, and generate any text in seconds.

85. http://Gling.ai → AI video editor. Our AI will cut silences, and bad takes for you so you can focus on your YouTube videos

86. http://Rytr.me → AI copywriter. Rytr is an AI writing assistant that helps you create high-quality content, in just a few seconds, at a fraction of the cost!

87. http://Beautiful.ai → AI presentation software for the workplace

88. https://fireflies.ai. AI meeting assistant that uses NLP to eliminate the need for note-taking during a meeting.

89. https://www.usechatgpt.ai. Use ChatGPT (Plugins & GPT-4), Bard, Bing Chat, and Claude on any website without copy-pasting. Write, rewrite, summarize, translate, explain, or reply to any text everywhere with one click.

90. https://monica.im.. Your ChatGPT Powered AI Assistant on All Websites

91. https://wiseone.io Helps you master any topic you read online by bringing relevant and reliable information.

92. https://www.compose.ai Write Faster With AI, Save Time. Compose AI is a Chrome extension that cuts your writing time by 40% with AI-powered autocompletion & text generation.

93. https://www.stork.ai. AI-Based Collaboration for Hybrid Teams Rich media messaging, advanced video and voice conferencing, auto-transcribing, and screen sharing.

Serendipitous meetings at the water cooler with your human and AI teammates.

94. http://Typedesk.com Save time everywhere you work. Create text shortcuts that work across all your apps and websites for all your repetitive text content

95. http://Chatgpt4google.com Supercharge Google w/ ChatGPT. ChatGPT response alongside search engine results.

96. https://gencraft.com. The world's most powerful AI photo and video art generation engine. What will you create?

97. https://kaiber.ai Tell stories like never before with our advanced AI generation engine to create video from the text.

98. https://stunning.so. Build websites with AI

99. https://metrotechs.io/ artificial intelligence and performance-oriented web hosting to help launch and scale your brand online.

100. https://chatronai.com/ Unique AI Content, Image, and Codes Generator

My goal was to give you insightful knowledge and practical advice for using ChatGPT successfully. I am confident you can create worthwhile passive income streams and succeed in this business environment by following the best practices described in this book and the applicable procedures.

How would Warren Buffer close out this book? Let's ask ChatGPT...

THIS FINAL CHAPTER PROVIDES A SUMMARY OF THE BOOK'S KEY INSIGHTS, INCLUDING THE SIGNIFICANCE OF UTILIZING CHATGPT FOR CREATING PASSIVE INCOME STREAMS, RECOGNIZING ITS LIMITATIONS, AND IMPLEMENTING BEST PRACTICES FOR SUCCESS. THE CHAPTER ALSO PROVIDES ACTIONABLE STEPS THAT READERS CAN TAKE TO ACHIEVE SUCCESS WITH CHATGPT, SUCH AS SETTING CLEAR OBJECTIVES, CONSISTENTLY PRACTICING AND REFINING THEIR USE OF THE TOOL, AND REGULARLY EVALUATING THEIR PROGRESS. BY FOLLOWING THESE METHODS, READERS WILL BE ABLE TO EFFECTIVELY HARNESS THE POWER OF CHATGPT TO INCREASE THEIR PRODUCTIVITY AND GENERATE A SUSTAINABLE ONLINE INCOME.

Thank You

You could have picked from hundreds of other books, but you bought mine, and I appreciate it. Thank you so much for purchasing my book.

Not that you enjoyed (I hope) my book, can I ask you for a tiny favor? Can you please post a review on the platform? You posting a review is the best way to support the work of independent authors like me.

Your feedback will help me keep writing the books that will help you get the desired results. It means a lot to me to hear from you.

I am happy for anyone to reach out to me for help, comments, collaboration ideas, or feedback at

brian@brianscottfitzgerald.com

Visit my author page with this link or Scan this QR code

https://www.amazon.com/author/brianscottfitzgerald.

Thank You